P9-DYD-710

GOOD OLD DAYS® REMEMBERS

Working on the Farm™

Edited by Ken and Janice Tate

HOUSE of
WHITE
BIRCHES

PUBLISHERS
SINCE 1947

Good Old Days Remembers Working on the Farm

Copyright © 2000 House of White Birches, Berne, Indiana 46711

All rights reserved. No part of this publication may be reproduced or transmitted in any form or by any means, electronic or mechanical, including photocopying, recording, or any other information storage and retrieval system, without the written permission of the publisher.

Editors: Ken and Janice Tate
Associate Editor: Barb Sprunger
Copy Editors: Läna Schurb, Mary Nowak

Production Coordinator: Brenda Gallmeyer
Design/Production Artist: Beverly Jenkins
Cover Design: Jessi Butler
Traffic Coordinator: Sandra Beres
Production Assistants: Janet Bowers, Marj Morgan, Chad Tate
Photography: Tammy Christian, Jeff Chilcote
Photography Assistant: Linda Quinlan
Photography Stylist: Arlou Wittwer

Publishers: Carl H. Muselman, Arthur K. Muselman
Chief Executive Officer: John Robinson
Marketing Director: Scott Moss
Product Development Director: Vivian Rothe
Publishing Services Manager: Brenda Wendling

Customer Service: (800) 829-5865

Printed in the United States of America
First Printing: 2000
Library of Congress Number: 00-132489
ISBN: 1-882138-64-3

Every effort has been made to ensure the accuracy of the material in this book. However, the publisher is not responsible for research errors or typographical mistakes in this publication.

We would like to thank the following for the art prints used in this book:

Apple Creek Publishing: *Daddy's Little Helper* by Charles Freitag, page 95.
For information on art prints, contact Apple Creek Publishing, Hiawatha, IA 52233, (800) 662-1707.

Mill Pond Press: *Bountiful Harvest* by Jim Daly, front cover; *Homemade* by Jim Daly, page 54;
Wash Day by Jim Daly, page 79; *Harvest Supper* by Don Spaulding, page 83; *Timeless Summer* by Jim Daly, page 131;
Tranquil Moments by Jim Daly, page 139; and *Polly & Jake* by Luke Beck, page 145.
For information on art prints, contact Mill Pond Press, Venice, FL 34292, (800) 535-0331.

Wild Wings Inc.: *Apple Picking* by Lee Stroncek, page 19; *New Shoes* by Lee Stroncek, page 24;
Wheat Harvest by Hal Sutherland, page 32; *Spring* by Lee Stroncek, page 92; *Blueberry Picking* by Lee Stroncek, page 114;
Clear Creek Morning by Chris Cummings, page 121; and *A Fence to Be* by Hal Sutherland, pages 126, 127.
All by arrangement with Wild Wings Inc., Lake City, MN 55041, (800) 445-4833.

We would also like to give a very special thank you to *Swiss Heritage Village*, Berne, Ind., pages 15 and 67,
and Berne Public Library for use of the photograph on page 160.

Dear Friends of the Good Old Days,

Back on the farm in the Good Old Days we all knew what it meant to work. Janice and I both grew up on farms in the Ozark Mountains, and there spent our young lives learning what it means to toil. Janice was the only child in her family and did the work of both sons and daughters in the family's dairy from the time she was barely big enough to take care of calves. I was the middle of three children, and worked long and hard in the fields and milk barn of our own hard-scrabble farm.

There was great satisfaction in working on the farm, whether you were man, woman or child. With our faithful farm animals we tilled the soil, cultivated crops and reaped what we sowed in heartfelt gratitude and thanksgiving. I have often said it was easier to be close to our Creator in those days. After all, we were immersed every day in His creation, and we thought of ourselves in a sort of partnership with Him. We worked hard with what He had given us and were never miserly with the increase He provided.

My favorite time of year was—and still is—the fall. As the days shortened our work days, and the crisp autumn air marked the end of harvest, all of us farm folks were able to take a collective sigh of relief. Crops were all in and we could pause a bit to enjoy the fruits of our labors. Oh, yes, there was a hard winter ahead of caring for stock and doing all the little things around the farm that planting, growing and harvest seasons never permitted. But there was a peaceful exhilaration about the fall.

One of my favorite poems, *When the Frost Is on the Punkin* by James Whitcomb Riley, sums it up better than I could:

> "The husky, rusty russel of the tossels of the corn,
> And the raspin' of the tangled leaves, as golden as the morn;
> The stubble in the furries—kindo' lonesome-like, but still
> A-preachin' sermuns to us of the barns they growed to fill;
> The strawstack in the medder, and the reaper in the shed;
> The hosses in theyr stalls below—the clover overhead!—
> O, it sets my hart a-clickin' like the tickin' of a clock,
> When the frost is on the punkin and the fodder's in the shock!"

It's perhaps hard for youngsters today to understand how all of us could enjoy working from dawn to dusk, six days a week. They might even think we were at least deprived, if not abused, in such hard-working families. If truth be told, we were blessed.

Travel with us back to those Good Old Days on the farm. These real-life stories will take you back to the time when families stood shoulder to shoulder, working against Depression, dearth and drought to build a better life together. Those days of Working on the Farm were really the best days of our lives.

Ken Tate

❧ Contents ❧

"Man May Work ..." • 7

"But a Woman's Work ..." • 53

Children's Chores • 93

Help From the Barnyard • 133

"Man May Work ..."

❧❧❧

One quality I inherited from my father is that of being an early riser. "The early bird always gets the worm," he told me over and over again when I was a youngster. I never knew what could be considered good about getting the worm, but I learned as a young bird that I wanted it.

Daddy was always up well before first light, moving around in the kitchen and setting the pot on the stove for his morning coffee. The noise usually awakened me, and I stumbled into the kitchen with bleary eyes wondering what Daddy was doing.

Usually I was ordered back to bed with a stern, "Coffee will stunt your growth, boy." But once in a while my father poured me a glass of milk, pushed out a chair at the table and allowed me a brief glimpse into his early morning life.

We had no morning newspaper, but there was always plenty to talk about. Maybe it was the baseball game we had listened to on the radio the night before. Perhaps the war or the economy was the topic of the morning. Many times the conversation centered on the work of the day ahead—cows to milk, weeds to hoe, green beans to pick, snap and prepare for Mama's canner. I figured out where that worm was that we early birds were supposed to get—the cottonpickin' thing was either in our garden or barn lot, challenging me to brave the dew-drenched summer morning to look for him.

By the time our chats were finished, yellow strands of daybreak were streaming in the east window, silhouetting father and son on the drab kitchen wallpaper.

"Dawn is my favorite time of day," Daddy always told me, "because it's a new day. If you're up at dawn and work hard every day, good things will happen."

So dawn became my favorite time of day, too. In the twilight before sunrise I recognize the hope each new day brought my father. "Man may work from sun to sun ..." starts the old adage—and from Daddy I learned that working from daylight to dark is a good and honorable thing.

Now our bedroom faces east, and the July sun comes up pretty early in the morning. I know it probably drives Janice crazy, but I still can't stay in bed past sunrise, even if sunrise is at 5 a.m. We don't have a clock in the bedroom, because my internal alarm goes off before the sun breaks the horizon.

"Early to bed, early to rise, makes a man healthy, wealthy and wise." I don't know that the practice has made me all that wealthy, but Janice always knew that she and the children would be provided for. I don't know that I was made all that wise, either, but I have been blessed with pretty good health. One out of three isn't bad, I guess.

And now that I have the perspective of age, I'm glad Daddy taught me to be an early bird—whether I wanted the worm or not. These stories of farmers who, like Daddy and I, were early risers will make you smile as you remember those long days of work in the Good Old Days.

—*Ken Tate*

Farmer's Lament

By Don Lacey

Farmers, they all have it made,
Some city folks still say,
But I wish they'd trail along with me
For just one farming day.

The alarm clock started clanging
And I jumped right out of bed;
The bureau drawer was open
And I banged it with my head.

I grabbed a cup of coffee;
It was a trifle hot.
I singed my lips and boiled my tongue,
And it will bother, like as not.

I rushed to feed the cattle
Out where my haystacks stand.
I stumbled over my pitchfork
And ran it through my hand.

So I went down to the pasture
To stretch some sagging fence;
The rusty wire, it parted,
And my arm's been different since.

Then I walked across my cornfield
To ponder at the crust.
I viewed a million bugs a-chewing,
And I knew 'twould be a bust.

I jumped onto my tractor
To make another round,
But it made a fearful noise
When that rod began to pound.

So I went to see my banker
To float another loan.

He stared at me in silence
And his face resembled stone.

Said cattle prices were falling
And farm costs way too high,
So with this new threat of foreclosure
I may be leaving by and by.

In my yard I have a rose bush.
A bee was waiting there.
It soon became quite tricky
To sit upon a chair.

So, for nerve tonic, I went fishing,
Down where the old Platte flows,
But I felt a little foolish
With that fishhook in my nose.

Then I made myself a promise:
This thing was going to end.
I'd rent my blasted weed patch
To some unsuspecting friend.

Then I'd hie me to the mountains
And I'd spend the summer there,
And for that poor misguided fellow,
I'd breathe a silent prayer.

But fools are made to blunder
And so I'll carry on,
And subsidize this nightmare
And be its silly pawn.

You say I am a fibber?
Well, yes, I stretched it a bit,
But come, try your hand at farming,
And you'll never censor it.

Life at the Old Mill

By Melvin Kay

I was brought up in an old-time flour and feed mill, located in a deep valley in the hills of western Maryland. The old-fashioned country water mill is now a thing of the past, seen only on Christmas cards and calendars. But I have many fond memories of the mill.

What fascinated me most was the great overshot waterwheel that supplied the mill's power. "Overshot" refers to the way the water overshot the top of the waterwheel by means of a flat trough and fell into the "buckets" on the front of the wheel, slowly turning it by the sheer weight of the water.

The high wheel turned very slowly, about the same speed as the Ferris wheel at the fairgrounds. As the water reached the bottom of the wheel, it poured out into the stream under the wheel. It is the sound of the water, dripping, pouring and gurgling its way around the wheel, that I have never forgotten. I still make running models of these old overshot waterwheels, and as I watch them run, I go back in memory to those fond days of long ago.

The old-time waterwheel was made of wood and its top reached almost to the eaves at the gable end of the mill. Its axle was a huge wooden shaft, hand-hewn from a tree trunk. This large shaft turned a high wooden cogwheel just inside the mill, and the sound of this cog as it meshed with the other wooden cogs could be heard all through the valley.

Mother would look down the little country road from the old millhouse window and exclaim, "Here comes Mr. Jones to the mill; I know his team."

Water to run the wheel was channeled from a dam by means of the millrace. When I was a small child, I would go with my father at the end of the day to watch him drop wet sawdust around the wheel gate so that no water would be lost during the night.

Not far above the mill dam was "the old swimmin' hole." We had always managed to discard our clothes on the run by the time we reached it; bathing suits were unknown. We were much put out when the girls wanted to swim too, inspiring someone to put up the sign "No Bathing Without Suits."

When summer thunderstorms came, the old millstream could quickly rise up to the banks. Dad rushed into his rain togs and rubber boots to set

the floodgates in place at the upper end of the millrace. They kept the high water from flooding the lower part of the mill.

Farmers brought their grain to the mill in wagons pulled by one, two or four horses. I could not tell one team from another, but Mother would look down the little country road from the old millhouse window and exclaim, "Here comes Mr. Jones to the mill; I know his team." As the years passed and horse-drawn wagons gave way to cars and trucks, Mother felt lost indeed; one truck looked like another to her.

In winter, when the mill road was deep in snow, wagons gave way to large homemade sleds. They made a picture never to be forgotten.

The teams brought wheat for flour, barley, corn and rye to be ground for horses and cows. Dad always "tested" the wheat before unloading it. First he held it under his nose. Then he threw a little of it into his mouth. If you saw a good miller "chewing," it could be wheat.

Most farmers stored their wheat at the mill for the winter. They were given a small book showing the amount of flour to be received for the wheat they left with the miller. Each time the farmer got his flour, it was noted in the book. Grain to be ground for feed was either paid for by the bushel, or "tolled"—that is, a 10th of a bushel was kept by the miller to pay for the grinding.

Grinding grain for cattle and horses was done on the "burrs," or millstones, two very heavy stones made of flint, 4–5 feet in diameter. The top stone rested and turned upon the bottom stone. Grain entered through an opening in the center of the top stone, and the turning stone slung it to the outer edge where it fell into a spout and then into the sack. The upper stone could be raised or lowered to obtain the proper texture.

The process was the same when grinding corn for cornmeal, except that the spout directed the meal to a "sifter" on the floor. The sifter was attached to an eccentric shaft that shook the contraption back and forth, separating hulls from meal. I could never forget the fragrance of that

warm, fresh meal; it looked like a small mountain of finely ground gold and conjured up visions of corn pone hot out of the old-fashioned oven.

When making buckwheat flour, the black, sharp-edged buckwheat grain was fed into the stone burr and a finer sieve was slipped into the sifter. Buckwheat flour was finer in texture, of course, and had a rich, dark color all its own. It made me think of large, brown, plate-size buckwheat cakes covered with sausage gravy, which were our main breakfast fare during the long winter months.

One of the big jobs in the old-fashioned mill was "dressing" or sharpening these heavy and cumbersome millstones. The arm of a large wooden derrick was swung over the top stone

Sometimes I would open the office door to find Dad asleep on the old dusty couch with a tattered Bible on his chest, open to the place where he had been reading.

and lifted high enough so that when it was turned, the grinding surface was on top. The grinding surfaces of both the upper and lower stones had to be "dressed" or made rough enough to grind grain. The sparks flew when specially tempered sharp hammers were used to cut new grooves into the grinding surfaces. This "dressing" took several days.

Wheat flour was made with rollers instead of millstones. The grain was fed between two steel rollers, one running faster than the other. The sifting was done with "bolting clothes"; very fine in mesh and made of silk, they formed a large cylinder that turned around and around. The fine flour sifted through and the coarser material was returned to the rollers to be ground again.

The roller mill produced three products when processing the wheat: the flour, fine in texture and very white; the bran from the outer hull of the wheat; and the "middlings," or wheat germ. People ate the flour, cows ate the bran, and pigs ate the middlings.

Whole-wheat flour was little known in those days, but once in a great while, Dad got a call for it. The method he used to produce it was very simple. He simply milled the flour as usual, then recombined the flour, bran and middlings in the proper proportions. Later on

he occasionally received a request for wheat germ. He simply caught the middlings in a sack before they were ground fine.

Old-time millers didn't bleach their flour, but they did take great pride in producing a fine grade of flour. They tested it for whiteness with a "flour slick," a small, flat piece of shiny metal that the miller carried in his pocket. By passing the flour slick over some flour he held in his hand, he could easily see "specks" in his flour. If too many showed up, the mill was stopped and any holes in the silk bolting clothes were repaired.

If a farmer returned flour and complained that it would not make good bread, Dad refilled Mother's flour bucket with it without telling her. Mother was a splendid baker. If the flour made rich, brown loaves (and it usually did), Dad knew his flour was not at fault.

One problem that plagued the old-time miller was the "choke-up." The mill was interlaced with a system of wooden spouts that carried ground wheat from the rollers to the elevators and from the elevators to the bolting clothes. These spouts sometimes became choked, and then elevators stopped, belts flew off and the whole milling process was thrown out of kilter. That's when an experienced miller showed his skill. He released the contents of the choked spouts onto the floor and tapped other spouts with wooden hammers or rammed them clear with long rods until normal flow resumed. A good miller could always tell by the sound of his mill when a choke-up was brewing.

There was, of course, no heating system in the old mill, and in the winter, the building was bitterly cold. The only way to keep warm was by making frequent trips to the mill office, where a small "chunk" stove was kept hot by corncobs from the corn sheller. In the office was an old sofa, saturated with mill dust, which Dad used for frequent naps, for his hours were long. Many times I awakened before daylight to hear the mill running, and it was the last sound I heard when I dropped off to sleep at night. Sometimes I would open the office door to find Dad asleep on the old dusty couch with a tattered Bible on his chest, open to the place where he had been

reading. We tiptoed away silently; the mill office was a haven of rest in more ways than one for a tired, dusty miller.

There were none of the many safety devices such as those that are required today, but even though we used the mill from basement to attic as a playground, we usually escaped unharmed. (The angels were with us.) Some of the things that happened, however, scared the wits out of me.

Most vivid is my memory of the time I was playing with the hoist rope near the outside door

on the third floor. This rope was used to hoist sacks of grain from the wagons below to the upper floors of the mill. On this occasion it was not a sack of grain, but me that was hoisted, when the hook on the end of the rope caught me by the seat of my pants and pulled me out of the door. There I hung, dangling in space! Down I would go as my weight pulled on the rope, then up I would rise as the control rope, which I still held in one hand, tightened again. The mill was running, but somehow, Dad heard me yell! Never was I more glad to see my dad!

I came to know the sights, sounds and smells of the great old mill in many ways, but in one way in particular did every nook and corner of the mill become known to me. I asked Dad if I might have the job of sweeping the mill! I was delighted when he said I could, but it was with great hesitation that I asked him about wages. Could he pay me, say, 5 cents a week?

So it came about that my first real job was in the mill, and how I hoarded those nickels! I saved every one in a tiny pitcher on the old-fashioned sideboard in our home.

It's no wonder that life in the old mill became so much a part of me. Now that I am retired, I find myself here in the valley where I played as a boy, starting in just where I left off so long ago! ❖

The Broom Maker

By Joanne M. Schlegal

My parents lived on a small farm and my father did all the farming with three horses. There were five children, four girls and one boy.

It was in 1924 that my father decided he would like to make and sell brooms. In the spring, he planted a small patch of broomcorn seed. That summer, he made himself a hand-powered machine to make the brooms.

When harvesttime came, we were all excited, except for my mother. She felt there could be no money in broom making.

Father cut the tops off the broomcorn and laid them out in the barnyard to dry. After three days, he stripped the seed off, and he was ready to make the first broom.

When we came home from school that day, there was the broom he had made—but it didn't look like a broom. It was too thick. Mother said, "I knew you couldn't make a broom."

The next day he went to a broom factory about 10 miles from our farm. He stayed there all day.

When he cut more broomcorn, he didn't let it dry as long as the first cutting. His first broom was yellow and it was supposed to be green.

Several days later, he made another broom. It looked a whole lot better. He sewed through the bristles with a long needle, making four rows of stitching. Then he trimmed the ends of the boom straws to make them even.

He presented the finished broom to Mother. She swept the floor, and we all had a good laugh.

It wasn't long before word got around that he could make brooms. People brought their broomcorn to him, and more people started to raise it. He put out 2 or 3 acres himself.

He sold his brooms for 75 cents apiece. He was 46 years old when he started making brooms, and he did that work for 34 years and reaped a nice profit.

Children loved him because he made small, children-size brooms just for them and gave them away. They looked forward to his arrival as he made his rounds.

Father lived to be 90 years old. I often think about those Good Old Days, when he was my father, the broom maker. ❖

The Ice Harvest

By A.W. Ranniger

s a young boy, I looked forward to my summertime visits to my grandparents' farm. Even in those days, grandparents doted on their grandchildren, and a visit always started off with homemade cookies and cold lemonade. Since the farm had no electricity or refrigerator, an ice-cold drink was a satisfying treat, made possible by the wooden icebox that stood in the corner of the big farm kitchen.

The icebox was an insulated wooden chest of finished oak with two compartments. Food in the lower compartment was cooled by chunks of ice in the top compartment. As the ice thawed, the water drained into a drip pan under the chest. Regular filling of the ice container and emptying of the icebox drip pan were small efforts for the returns.

The wooden icebox was one of the luxuries of its time. Without an icebox, the only way to keep perishable foods such as butter from spoiling was to place such items in a bucket and hang the bucket in the coolness of a well. A small well topped by a hand-operated pump was often located close to the kitchen door. When such a pump was not available, it was common to dig a posthole to water level and hang perishable items in it.

Of course, without ice, the wooden icebox became just a wooden chest. To have ice in the summertime, one had to harvest ice in the winter. This was always exciting and invigorating. February, when the ice was usually thickest, was the time to hitch the team of horses to the family bobsled and head to the slough or neighboring pond or river. There, with the help of neighbors and relatives, the ice would be harvested for next summer's use.

A long, large-tooth saw would be inserted into a hole chopped in the ice. The ice was then cut into checkerboard squares. The men took turns using the saws. There would be talk about using a large circular saw

blade (used for cutting family firewood) and building a portable ice-cutting rig. It remained just talk. Most ice blocks were cut by hand instead of engine.

Besides the saws, other ice-harvesting tools were jack poles and ice tongs. The jack poles were long poles with hooks or spikes on one end. They were used to steer floating ice blocks into open water. The men grabbed the ice blocks from the water with large metal ice tongs. Once a block of ice was grabbed, it would require a little push down into the water. The water resistance and upward force on the block of ice helped the harvester pull it up out of the water.

Once the ice blocks were pulled out of the water, they were placed on end to help freeze the ice dry. When enough ice had been harvested, it was loaded onto the sleds for the trip back to the farmstead and the icehouse. In the icehouse, the chunks of ice were arranged in even layers.

Ice chips were filled in between the blocks to help freeze them together. Sawdust was poured on top and around the edges of each layer. A horse and pulley hoisted the heavy blocks of ice to the upper parts of the icehouse. When the building was full, another 3 feet of sawdust was added to the top for insulation.

Summer heat and frequent trips to the icehouse with an ice pick and ice bucket gradually reduced the huge mound of ice, but there would usually be enough to make ice cream for the July Fourth celebration.

And there would always be ice to make cool lemonade for grandchildren—even if it meant a trip to town to purchase a block of ice for the old wooden icebox. ❖

Old Home Orchard

By J. Marshall Porter

*M*ost of us who spent our early years on a farm cannot help but think fondly now and then of the old home orchard.

When I was growing up, every family farm had an orchard. Large or small, it was as much a part of the farm as the home garden, and far more important, because most of the apples and other fruits were marketed as cash crops.

There were about 100 full-grown trees in the orchard of our home farm. My grandfather had set them more than 30 years before I was born. All were seedlings to which he had budded or grafted the best varieties of that day and locality.

Grandfather knew nothing about spraying, but he knew that worms and insects were harmful to the trees and fruit. He worked burnt lime into the ground above the roots, reasoning that lime would kill most insects and worms that came in contact with it. Each spring he whitewashed the trunks and low limbs as high as he could reach. The orchard bloomed pink and white above those newly whitewashed trunks and limbs.

Grandfather pruned and shaped the trees as they were growing. He kept them low and wide, and their limbs nearly met in the rows, which were too narrow. He loved that orchard and gave it tender, loving care. He was rewarded with many bountiful crops. When his health began to fail in the latter part of his last winter, he spoke frequently of hoping to live to see the orchard bloom again. We thought it a miracle, but he did.

My father loved that orchard, too. He knew how Grandfather had cared for it, and he followed the same methods. But fire, blight and age began taking their toll. He pruned out the blighted limbs and cut back some of the living ones, and new wood grew and made young trees on old trunks. Some of those trees lasted many years; others broke and fell from the hollow trunks when heavily laden with fruit.

As the old trees broke or died out, father set new nursery trees in their place. My earliest recollection of working with him is of holding the young trees straight while he shaped the roots in the holes he had dug, then shoveled the soil on top.

In later years, I also set trees in that orchard as the old ones died out. Thus, three generations of our family set trees, cared for them and gathered abundantly from their fruitful limbs. We learned, too, that trees, like men, have their seasons of life: their spring, or time of growing; their summer of full fruitfulness; their autumn of waning strength; and their winter, when they are no longer productive.

In the days when home orchards supplied the fruit for nearby towns and villages, it was customary for farmers to exchange buds and grafts of their favorites.

Many varieties grew in our orchard. Early Harvest was a rich, yellow-fleshed apple that ripened in mid-July. From these, our womenfolk baked tasty pies and sent them to the harvest fields as an afternoon refreshment for the harvesters. Golden Sweet was becoming mellow for eating about the time we hauled grain and hay into the barn. They were a delight to hungry boys working in fields and mows. We also had varieties including Early Rambo, Smokehouse Baldwin, McIntosh, yellow and black Bellflower, Russets and Northern Spy, and some excellent-flavored

fruit that I have never found in any other orchard. We had names for them, but likely they were seedlings.

In the days when home orchards supplied the fruit for nearby towns and villages, it was customary for farmers to exchange buds and grafts of their favorites. Grafts usually began bearing in their third year.

The apple crop was no small part of the conversation when neighbors met at the store, mill, blacksmith shop and even in the churchyard. The crop supplied a goodly part of the family food then, for every family made a large kettle of apple butter each fall. Many a romance began at apple cuttings, when neighbors went to each other's homes to help cut up the apples the night before the boiling was to begin. After the older folks had tired from a long day of stirring, the young folks went out in couples to stir under the stars with only the kettle fire for light. Gay, youthful voices mingled with the sounds of crickets and katydids as the boiling kettle bubbled and splashed about the long-handled ladle.

Most farmers had their own cider mill, and the family worked hard to gather the windfalls and culls into large burlap bags to be hauled in for cider making. This was an after-school and Saturday task for most farm youngsters. I helped pick up fallen apples when I was still too short to walk without dragging my picking basket. What a delight it was to watch as the apples were ground and pressed on the old hand-powered mill.

All farmers stored barrels of cider in their cellars or outbuildings. They served it to visitors with spice cake as a refreshment in various degrees of hardness. It was usually very hard by butchering time. But everyone knew a method for keeping cider sweet over the winter. Some dropped a piece of lean, raw beef into the barrel. Later, preservatives could be bought in drugstores. Oil of wintergreen, teaberry, peppermint or sassafras made a fine-flavored drink until the

barrel was empty. Others pasteurized the cider by boiling and filtering it, then storing it in kegs and jugs. Good vinegar was made by filling a barrel with cider made from ripe apples. The waste, or "workings," was allowed to escape through the bunghole. It was kept from hard freezing.

Most varieties of apples then were biennial bearers. The owners of home orchards did not know that while the tree was growing its crop through August, it also had to produce the buds that made the next crop. In later years, orchardists learned that fertilizer, principally nitrate of soda and sulfate of ammonia, applied over the roots each spring at the rate of a few pounds per tree, would supply the food and energy the trees needed to produce a crop of fruit annually.

Gradually, fruit from home orchards began to show more and more effects of disease and insect damage. When the well-sprayed graded fruit from commercial orchards was displayed in grocery stores and markets, the gnarled and wormy homegrown fruit was no longer marketable. Owners of small home orchards could not afford to buy spraying equipment and material for the limited amount of fruit they produced, and they began to direct their efforts toward other products and crops. The useless fruit was left to rot beneath the trees, and that made it more difficult for the trees to survive. Trees in most of these orchards have died out or have grown thick and bushy. Many orchards have been cut or dozed out altogether. They will not return, for apple growing is a scientific, specialized business now, and only the most efficient operators can keep going year after year.

Fond memories of our old home orchard tangle around my heart and dreams, as the bittersweet and ivy vines tangle around the dying Rambo and Northern Spy trees that stand fruitless. The land could be used for more profitable crops, but I find it hard to sentence them to be torn from the earth that nurtured them for so many years. ❖

Truck Gardening

By Floyd Balmer as told by Barbara Roderick

In the early 1920s, growing up on a farm in southern Michigan, we farmed with horses. "We" included my mother, father, five brothers and three sisters, who moved from Paulding County, Ohio, in 1915 when I was 4 years old.

Money wasn't plentiful; with 11 mouths to feed, a garden was a necessity. Thus came the cash-generating project of truck gardening.

Truck gardening is what farmers do to get fresh fruits and vegetables to your table. Back in the mid-to late 1920s, there was little machinery available to help plant, cultivate and harvest crops. That is where we kids got involved. Those who were old enough to drive horses plowed the fields and cultivated the beans, corn, tomatoes, potatoes, etc. The rest of us hoed. This was an all-day, everyday project.

When my father bought a 2-ton truck, he reasoned that if we needed to raise a garden for our family anyway, why couldn't it be expanded to raise fruits and vegetables to sell? Our farm was about 50 miles from Detroit's Eastern Market. Why not take our produce there to sell?

The truck garden grew to encompass several acres. As the produce ripened, it had to be picked. To ensure fresh produce, this could not be done too far in advance. The Eastern Market was open every day of the week, with the biggest selling day on Saturday.

My father and older brother left home each morning at 2 a.m. to be at the market by 5 a.m., where they sold the day's load of produce. While they were at the market, and later, when they were home sleeping, the rest of us kept busy hoeing, picking vegetables, and dressing chickens we had bought from a neighbor to send to market to sell.

Some of us were sent to the large huckleberry marsh on our farm to pick huckleberries for market, too. Once I picked 48 quarts in one day. The mosquitoes and snakes were plentiful, and there was rumored to be a bear in those parts. But the mosquitoes were the worst; if a snake got in our basket, we just tossed him out.

We sold the berries in the same wooden quart boxes we used for cherries. But the slats in the corners were too big for huckleberries, so we put strips of paper in the corners to make them tight.

We gathered any product we could sell. In the fall we gathered elderberries and wild grapes and made them available to the wine makers in Detroit to produce homemade wine (this was during Prohibition).

Back in the mid-to-late '20s, there was little machinery available to help plant, cultivate and harvest crops. That is where we kids got involved.

Occasionally, a customer would bring a sample to our truck.

The Eastern Market was our schoolroom in the summer. We quickly learned to barter and make change. Since money was scarce and we needed shoes for the fall, we all got good at these skills. Usually only two or three of us kids got to go to the market, so we took turns. Those at home hoed and did the other farm work, like making hay to feed the horses.

The day the state sales tax law went into effect was the last day we trucked to the Eastern Market. My father could not be bothered to figure a percentage of the purchase and add that to the total for our retail customers. There were too many forms to fill out and send in as well. ❖

Neighborhood "Vet"

By Edna P. Bates

My father had no formal degree. He didn't have a chance to go to a university—or even to high school, for that matter. At 14, he became a full-time farmer, out of necessity. His father was an invalid; someone had to run the farm, and being the older son, he was elected.

His "degree" was not merely an honorary one, and he earned it in the hardest school of all: the school of experience. My father was Enos Jeffery, M.F.—Master of Farming!

He had to be a knowledgeable mechanic to fix all the farm machinery. He was a mender—with a needle, an awl, a hammer, some tacks and a shoe last, he half-soled, heeled and sewed up the rips in our family's footwear. He used the same equipment plus some copper rivets and a small anvil to repair the horses' harness.

He had to learn to be an arborist, to find out which kinds of trees grew best on the different kinds of land on our farm. He had to learn a fair amount of chemistry in order to understand government bulletins and find out what kind of sprays would control fungi, insects and so forth.

One pig I remember, named Oinky, was fed by hand. He came dancing to the end of the pen, squealing loudly, anytime a human came near!

He was a blacksmith of sorts, and a breeder and trader of horses, too—not for showing, riding or racing, but for working on the farm. It was only during the last 20 years of his farming life that he had a tractor. His horses were the best cared for and the best trained in the neighborhood.

He was a carpenter and a gardener, an economist and an efficiency expert.

But my father's best work was as the neighborhood veterinarian. Though he never attended veterinary college, he not only looked after his own animals, but also frequently served as the unpaid "vet" for lots of other folks as well. No matter how busy he was, he would leave his work to help a neighbor with a sick animal. He never received or expected payment. Nowadays, I suppose he wouldn't be allowed to practice animal medicine without a license, but in those days, nobody objected. Like my father, few of our neighbors could afford a veterinarian's fee unless it was a dire emergency. The number of cases my father looked after would have added up to a sizable amount in a year.

My father played midwife to our own mares, cows and sows. He spent many a cold winter night in the barn with a cow that was having a difficult birth, and thus saved a good calf, and even the cow, which might well have died without his timely help.

When a sow farrowed, he took each squealing pink piglet as it arrived and put it in a hamper so none would be laid on by the sow, or perhaps wander away and be chilled. He brought the hamper of little pigs into the kitchen, where their squeals would not upset the new mother, and using the pliers, he broke off their baby teeth. Otherwise they would bite as they nursed, and the huge sow might jump up and hurt her tiny offspring unintentionally.

Within a few days they had to be given powdered iron so they would not get anemia. This was also a kitchen job, requiring the help of one of us girls. While he held the squealer's mouth open, his assistant put a spoonful of the black stuff way back in its mouth so it could not spit it out! If the sow got "off her feed," she had to be dosed immediately, before her milk dried up and her dependents became "bottle babies." If she had more piglets than teats, we had to bottle-feed the extras.

One pig I remember, named Oinky, was fed by hand. It was no problem to find which of the dozen identical babies was Oinky. He came dancing to the end of the pen, squealing loudly, anytime a human came near!

I often helped him dose our horses, cows and pigs. First he fastened the animal's head up with a rope so it could not pull it down. Then a large bottle full of medicine was put into the side of its mouth. My father massaged the animal's throat to be sure it was swallowing. Sometimes dry Epsom salts were spooned back into a big pig's mouth and water was poured in to make sure it swallowed them. What a delightful dose!

One of the injuries that happened all too often was a cut teat, caused when a cow, trying to get up, managed to step on herself. This had to be cared for well or the cow might develop mastitis. Then the milk, from the infected quarter at least, would be lost for a time. In a bad case, the cow might have to be "dried up" and sold at a loss to the slaughterhouse. So every morning

and night for a week or more, the teat had to be treated, and she had to be milked very carefully and the milk kept separate for the cats.

Even chickens were not immune to medical problems. How well I remember one winter when our laying hens got roup! Egg production took a sudden drop. After dark every night, when all the hens were sleeping on their perches, the "doctor" and his young and not always willing assistant (me) came to dose them. With a purple mixture of water and potassium permanganate crystals, we swabbed out the putrid stuff in their throats. Ugh! I can still remember the smell! Then we put Royal Purple Roup Cure in their drinking water. (It wasn't purple. That was just a trade name.)

I won a leather-bound copy of Black Beauty in the only public-speaking contest I ever entered. My topic? Chicken raising—a subject I knew from the ground up.

As the unpaid neighborhood vet, my father usually traveled alone. However, one night we girls were allowed to go along to a friend's home on an emergency call. Their cows had eaten some weed out in the pasture that was apparently poisonous. It had caused painful and dangerous bloating. It was already too late for some of the poor animals when he arrived, but he managed to save the rest by piercing their hides with his trusty jackknife to let out the gas. It was a dangerous, last-ditch measure, but it saved several cows.

Though my father was a regular churchgoer, he would miss a service to help an animal in trouble. One time he rushed off, still dressed for church, to take a pear out of a cow's throat. (Cows have a habit of grabbing anything edible they can reach and swallowing it before it is properly chewed. They can bloat and die very quickly if it is not removed.) I always think of my father when I read Jesus' defense before the Pharisees when they condemned him for healing a man on the Sabbath: "Which of you shall have an ass or an ox fallen into a pit, and will straightway pull him out on the Sabbath day?" My father certainly would have, whether it was his or a neighbor's.

The usual method of eliminating the stuck pear or

apple was to put a stick inside a rubber hose and push the offending fruit on down. The hose kept the stick from injuring the cow's throat. Even this method failed once, but my father, not easily defeated, put his hand down the cow's throat, worked his fingers around the pear and pulled it out. The cow, most unappreciative of his help, snapped her teeth shut just as he pulled out the pear and tore off his thumbnail. It was very painful, but eventually he grew a new nail. However, it was much thicker than the original— a souvenir from a very ungrateful cow!

One of his surgical efforts was a total failure. Our dog was an intelligent collie, trained to work with the cattle and go to the road to bring in the daily paper. Mickey normally did not chase cars, but one day a tiny little car drove into the yard. Our dog obviously didn't recognize it as a car, and ran at it, barking furiously. He hit the headlight, and it broke, tearing one corner of his mouth. My father, with my rather unwilling help, undertook to sew up the gash. But Mickey didn't understand that this was for his own good, and struggled till he was let go. His mouth healed without benefit of surgery, but he always "grinned" much more widely on the right side of his mouth after that—a reminder that even the best vets have their failures.

My father even undertook to carry on his veterinary skills by remote control. One summer, he and my stepmother were going away for a week's holiday. Just before they were to leave, a good-sized pig got sick. He sat on its back and held its head up by the ears, and while its mouth was open wide to squeal, I threw the dry medicine into the back of its throat. He didn't think he should leave, but I assured him that we could manage quite well. I'd be the "pig sitter" and my 8-year-old son could put the medicine into the pig's mouth. This system worked fine at first, while the pig was quite sick. But one day the recovering pig gave me a ride around and around the pen before we could get the medicine in its mouth. I declared that it must be well enough to discontinue treatment.

Farmers are still very special people, as all too few people realize, but nowadays there aren't too many left like my father, Enos Jeffery, the neighborhood vet. ❖

The Two-Horse Walking Plow

By Henry Fischer

The plow was a primary instrument of civilization and was probably developed in Egypt; some of the oldest remains of agriculture have been found in the valley of the Nile.

The first plow was roughly fashioned from a forked tree and pulled by any available power, including humans. One branch served as the beam; the other was cut off and pointed, and the tail was trimmed to form a handle. We can see plows of this crude type pictured on Egyptian monuments.

Tillers of the soil all over the world kept experimenting to improve the plow, but it wasn't until centuries later that John Deere, a pioneer blacksmith in Grand Detour, Ill., fashioned the first successful steel moldboard plow in 1837.

These ancient plows merely stirred or loosened the soil.

In the late 18th century, a one-piece cast-iron plow was patented in New Jersey, but was unsuccessful; it wore out quickly and was expensive to replace. Later, a cast-iron plow in which the share, moldboard and landslide were cast in separate pieces was patented. This also failed.

Nearly all plows turned the furrow to the right. The point took the most wear and could be replaced by changing two bolts.

Deere's plow, which would scour in any kind of soil, played an integral part in the expansion and development of rural America, from tough Midwest prairie soil to rocky hillsides.

James Oliver of South Bend, Ind., invented the chilled plow. This tempered and strengthened the moldboard without detracting from its wearing and scouring capabilities. He began to manufacture plows in 1855 and developed many other devices to simplify and improve them.

The most popular size turned a furrow 12 inches wide and 4–7 inches deep. It was pulled by two oxen, horses or mules. The main frame was called a "beam." A small wheel in front could be adjusted up or down to control depth. The replaceable point penetrated the soil. A curved moldboard turned the soil upside down, and a vertical landslide ran against the unplowed land.

A wooden crossbar braced the plow's handles so the operator could control it. A small blade called a "coulter" ran above and ahead of the point to open the slice.

One Hundred Years Ago
John Deere Gave to the World the Steel Plow

THE year was 1837. The place, Grand Detour, Illinois. John Deere, the village blacksmith, had been challenged . . . His friend, Lewis Crandall, had threatened to "go back East if you can't build me a plow that'll scour."

John Deere was worried, for well he knew that Lewis Crandall's problem was the problem of the bustling West. He had heard the talk of sturdy pioneers up and down the wagon trails. "It's the richest soil that lies outdoors," they said. "But no plow'll ever turn it, once the sod is broken."

No need to tinker with the cast iron and wood plows brought from the East, concluded Deere. Only a plow with a highly-polished surface could scour its way through this sticky soil.

. . . A highly-polished surface, mused the blacksmith.

Fortunate, indeed, that the sun shone brightly the morning John Deere went to the community's sawmill to repair a broken shaft.

Its brilliant rays bounced from the polished surface of a broken saw blade into the alert eyes of John Deere. Wait . . . that's it . . . steel . . . steel for plows . . . no soil could stick to that smooth surface.

Day and night he worked, perfecting his great idea . . . building the plow of his dreams. Into the field he took it . . . back to his shop for changes . . . out again and back again, until he was sure it was right.

A memorable day it was when, surrounded by skeptics and well-wishers, John Deere turned a clean furrow with his new steel plow. He had conquered the prairie soil . . . he had given new hope to the pioneers of the West . . . he had made possible the permanent settling of a great agricultural empire.

Now, Lewis Crandall could stay and farm his rich acres.

*   *   *   *   *

Little did John Deere realize that his name was to be burned deep into the history of agricultural progress. Humble, yet proud of his workmanship . . . practical, yet with vision enough to sense the needs of the times, he built plows that set the standard of plow quality the world over.

"I'll never put my name on an implement that hasn't in it the best that is in me," John Deere once said. That was his ruling pride, the ideal which has guided the great organization that bears his name today.

Eleven great factories building equipment for every farming operation . . . branch houses in every principal farming area . . . thousands of dealers selling and servicing John Deere goods—these are the living, thriving monuments to the man who gave to the world the steel plow, one hundred years ago.

Nearly all plows turned the furrow to the right. The point took the most wear and could be replaced by changing two bolts. A new point cost about $2. When I plowed in the '20s, a new plow could be bought for about $20 at most hardware stores. We used an Oliver; Sears Roebuck sold a Banner.

As they pulled the plow, the animal on the right side walked in the furrow which made him appear smaller than his teammate. With one hand on each handle and the lines fastened together around his back, one under his left arm and the other atop his right shoulder, the plowman had some control over his team by merely twisting his shoulders.

He could plow his field by doing all four sides. This meant he made a left-hand quarter-turn at each corner, guiding the horse in a new direction each time as he wrestled the plow back and started a new 12-inch slice. Or he could plow the field in strips by tipping the plow onto its right side on the strip ends as he turned the team around.

He could start a field by plowing one furrow, then reversing direction and flowing on top of it. This was called a "back furrow." If he plowed so that the furrows fell opposite each other, the last one was called a "dead furrow." The ridge and valley in the field might be visible the next time the field was plowed, so the style would be reversed.

When I was about 10 years old and anxious to plow, my father warned me of two things: Never lean over the handles, because if it struck a stone it would throw the implement up and it could clip me under the chin; and never drop the plow on its point. Being too heavy for one person to lift, it was moved from barn to field on a wagon. To load it, one would bear down on the handles to get the wheel on the wagon bed, then lift the handles to swing the plow onto the wagon. It was unloaded in reverse.

Two acres of plowing was an average day's work. The monotony could be broken by finding Indian arrowheads or by collecting worms and grubs for a fishing trip.

When they first started turning the soil in the early spring, the horses, being soft from not having worked much all winter, would soon be ⁻ffing and sweating, so the driver would stop ⁻ s the team rested, he would turn himself

around inside the reins, sit back on the crossbar, fold his arms and plan the next day's work, daydream or just enjoy nature.

A straight plowed furrow with all the debris turned under was a point of pride with early pioneers. Today it seems unimportant. Farmers now realize that leaving some debris on the surface helps control wind and water erosion.

Rubber tires were developed for tractors in the '30s and smaller, affordable tractors were built, signaling the demise of the two-horse walking plow. About the only places they can be seen today are at horse-drawn "Plow Day" events or in antique shops. ❖

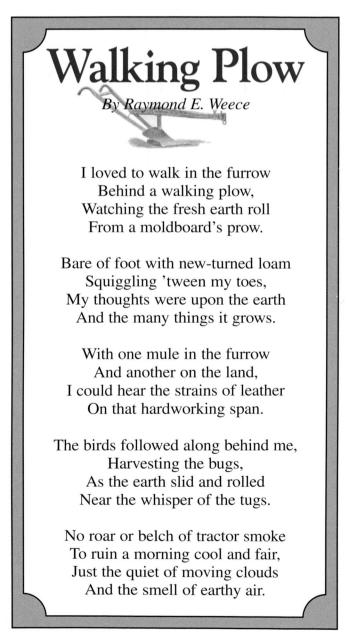

Walking Plow
By Raymond E. Weece

I loved to walk in the furrow
Behind a walking plow,
Watching the fresh earth roll
From a moldboard's prow.

Bare of foot with new-turned loam
Squiggling 'tween my toes,
My thoughts were upon the earth
And the many things it grows.

With one mule in the furrow
And another on the land,
I could hear the strains of leather
On that hardworking span.

The birds followed along behind me,
Harvesting the bugs,
As the earth slid and rolled
Near the whisper of the tugs.

No roar or belch of tractor smoke
To ruin a morning cool and fair,
Just the quiet of moving clouds
And the smell of earthy air.

Tobacco, Then and Now

By Laura Weddle

Today, "tobacco" is a dirty word, a catchall label that stands for the many unhealthy, antisocial, inconsiderate habits that people inflict upon themselves and others. Like chicken pox through a first-grade classroom, fear and loathing of the plant have infected the entire country. Restaurants, airlines, hospitals, colleges, even an entire city in California have become "smoke free."

And, I suppose, rightly so. There is no denying the ill effects of nicotine on health. I support initiatives to discourage the use of tobacco, and to abolish it in the workplace. Such initiatives are clearly giant steps toward a healthier, more energetic populace.

But I remember a time when the word "tobacco" had only positive connotations, for the necessities and pleasures of life—like food, shelter, clothes and Christmas joy.

My father was a tenant farmer in central Kentucky and our family's livelihood was derived from year-round cultivation of tobacco plants.

I remember walking barefoot to the tobacco beds on early spring mornings, the barely risen sun casting a white glow over the long, narrow canvas covers.

I remember my father carefully folding the covers back to expose the tender plants underneath. And I remember pulling them gently, one by one, laying them aside, protecting the tiny, hairlike roots that yearned to be planted in the cool brown soil.

When the plants had grown to a certain height and tobacco worms were clinging to the undersides of the leaves, it was my job, as the youngest and the shortest, to walk up and down the rows, pull off the clinging, feeding worms and smash them between my thumb and forefinger.

I loved this job because I knew what my daddy would say when I told him how many I'd killed. "That's good, Little Sugar," he'd say, whether I'd killed five or 50.

As I think about it, I can almost feel the sun and all the seasons of the crop's development: cool, almost chilly, on my arms in the early spring; stifling in the dog days of summer when the gum blackened my father's hands until even Lava soap wouldn't clean them; and the chill in the barn's stripping room when I stood close to the wood-burning stove while I graded the leaves and tried to stretch my short fingers to tie a hand of them.

Then, in early December—payoff time for the year's work—we would climb into the rafters of the barn, take down the sticks of pliable, pressed brown leaves, load them onto the bed of a wagon or pickup, and watch my father carry them away to market.

This was the time to settle the year's grocery bill, the time to buy huge bags of flour and cornmeal and 25-pound buckets of lard. Time to buy coats and shoes, or be given our older siblings' outgrown garments.

And it was also the time, with the money that remained, to buy bags of oranges and apples, hard, colorful, ribbon candy and a toy for each child to be hidden away until Christmas.

Part of me deplores the use of tobacco. It is the source of a dangerous drug that shortens lives and threatens the health of innocent bystanders. But there is another part of me—the child that I hope will never go—that hears the word "tobacco" and is immediately transported to a magical, sunny, ribbon-candy world. ❖

Threshing Days Remembered

By J. Marshall Porter

Threshing the grain crops on our small hill farms in western Maryland was about the most important event of the summer in 1910–1920, when I was growing up. There were six neighboring farms in our community and we all worked cooperatively to complete the threshing.

It was usually early August by the time our wheat, rye, barley and oats were harvested and hauled into the barns. Soon after that, we could expect the threshing machine to come, and when it did, we followed the cumbersome steam-powered traction engine and huge threshing machine from farm to farm. All the neighbors helped for help in return. Everyone who was big enough to do a little work of any kind was pressed into service.

It took 10–14 men to get the sheaves out of the barns and fed into the machine, the straw ricked, the grain measured and sacked and carried into the granary bins.

Those huge, cumbersome, noisy machines crawled over the steep, rocky lane that led to our farms. When they were well up the lane toward the farmyard, the engineer blew three blasts on the steam whistle to announce their coming. There were no telephones in our neighborhood yet.

The approach of threshing day meant a lot of work for everyone on the farm who was big enough to do any kind of work. It was a social time for those few who were too young or too old to work.

Long before daylight the threshermen were up and out, getting a fire started in the engine so as to have steam up to move the threshing machine.

"The threshermen," as the two who traveled with the machine were called, included the engineer, who drove the traction engine, and his helper. They spent the night at whichever farm they expected to thresh for the next day. If they arrived in time, they ate supper with the family. If it was late, the housewife would prepare supper for them unless they had eaten at their last stop.

As darkness settled amid the sounds of crickets, katydids and the calls of the midsummer whippoorwills from far back in the woods, the threshermen became part of the family, sitting on the vine-covered porch or lying in the warm grass of the farmyard. In most cases, they hadn't had a visit with the family since the previous year at threshing time. It was always a pleasant get-together, as the men discussed the weather conditions and crops and grain yields of the areas where they had already been. But the womenfolk rarely shared in such conversations; they were busy in the kitchen, preparing large quantities of food for the threshing crew the following day.

Before retiring, the engineer always carried a pail of water out to the engine and checked the fire he had raked from the engine's firebox when he had arrived. He knew that many fires started when winds arising during the night blew sparks into the dry hay and straw in the barns. He poured water over the pile of dying coals and went to bed, confident that no spark was left to cause disaster.

Long before daylight the next morning, the threshermen were up and out, getting a fire started in the engine so as to have steam up to move the threshing machine. The farmer was always consulted about this so as to set up in the handiest place to make the threshing job as easy as possible.

When the call came that "Breakfast is ready!" around sunrise, the traction engine was left standing and hissing steam, as if it was impatient to be getting on with the day's work. Breakfast at our place nearly always included big

One or two neighboring housewives often came to help prepare dinner and supper for the threshing crew.

platters of home-cured ham and fried eggs and lots of other good food to go with it. But there was never much lingering around the breakfast table; a hard day's work lay ahead.

The threshermen went directly to the barn and placed the measuring boxes, filled the water tanks of the engine and got up a good head of steam so as to be ready to start when all the helpers arrived.

Pretty soon the neighbors began arriving on foot. Nearly all of them carried pitchforks, ready to give their day's work. They knew they would be repaid in kind when the machine went to their farms. Nearly always a dog or two followed their masters, and refused to go home; a few fights could be expected every threshing day when strange dogs got together and disagreed about something.

A long, sagging belt with a half-twist was threaded from the threshing machine's small pulley to the large flywheel on the engine. When it was in place, a short trial run made sure everything worked properly—that the belts were tight and running true on the pulleys. As the machine went into motion, it emitted the grayish dust it had retained from the grain and weed seeds of previous threshings. Their aroma

blended with the smells of steam and oil—a pleasant fragrance, and anyone who ever knew it never forgot it.

When the engineer was satisfied that his machine was in good running order, he gave a Toot-toot! on the whistle. The men interpreted the signal to mean, "Let's thresh!" and the work began. Two men were needed to feed the machine, loading the sheaves headfirst into the revolving spiked cylinder. Other men were positioned in the barn to fork the sheaves out to the feeders.

The machine rumbled and groaned as it devoured the sheaves. Grain flowed out into measuring boxes that held a bushel each; these were tallied by the threshermen, who were paid by the bushel. Then the grain was emptied into

sacks, which were carried into the granary bins. The straw was blown out through a long steel pipe onto a big stack. It usually took two or three men to build the stack, giving it a peaked top that would keep rain from soaking in and spoiling the straw.

Until boys were at least 12, they were not considered big enough to work around the threshing machine, so they were given jobs such as carrying drinking water to the men and toting water for the steam engine. Depending on how far the water had to be carried and whether the path was level or steep, it could be very hard work indeed.

At our farm, the distance was a full 200 feet— and all uphill. At age 10, I pumped and carried a 2-gallon pail in each hand. Working hour after

hour, it became a very heavy load. But we didn't dare stop because the engine had to have great quantities of water. In later years, when I had grown enough to do a man's work, I learned that few jobs—if any—around the threshing machine were harder than carrying water.

Around 10 o'clock, some of the big girls or womenfolk would come from the house carrying a basket and a pail. At the sight of them, the engineer gave the whistle a toot, and the threshing came to a brief halt as the men refreshed themselves with generous wedges of apple or berry pie and lemonade. Faces dusty and shirts soaked through in dark patches under their arms and across their backs, the refreshed men were ready to resume threshing vigorously until dinnertime.

One or two neighboring housewives often came to help prepare dinner and supper for the threshing crew. Garden vegetables and orchard fruits were usually in abundant supply. Though their days were long and hot, it would have been hard to find better-fed men than those who helped thresh in our neighborhood.

Around noon, a long blast from the whistle announced that it was time to stop for dinner. The feeders stopped putting sheaves in the cylinder and the machine slowly came to a stop. Men came out of the barn, off the straw stack and away from whatever other jobs they were doing, and all headed toward the farmyard pump where several granite wash basins had been placed on a long bench along with a cube or two of homemade soap scented with sassafras root. A

half-dozen clean towels hung within handy reach. The pleasing aroma of food wafted out through the kitchen door to the hungry men as they washed up.

So that the meals didn't get monotonous, the farm wives planned their menus to vary from day to day, especially the meats. Spring chickens were ready to fry on most farms at that time of year and were freely served, though some housewives served roast beef or lamb, and others roasted or baked a home-cured ham.

The tables fairly groaned under the load of good food. But making it and eating it was a hot ordeal. In addition to the usual early August heat, there was the added heat from the stoves, making the kitchen almost unbearable—more so for the women who had to work there all day than for the men who only ate there.

At some of the farms where they had large porches, the tables were set up there. Others set the tables under shade trees in the yard.

Unless the crop was finished before late afternoon, the threshing crew ate supper before leaving a farm. It took hours to prepare the machine for the move to the next farm. Water tanks had to be filled, and the coal and wood boxes had to be filled on the engine. It was customary for each farmer to supply the coal, wood and water to take the threshing machine to the next farm.

If the threshermen thought they could get to the next farm before it became totally dark, they would move the machine that night. They carried no lights except two old battered lanterns. The farm lanes were narrow, steep and dangerous to travel with those cumbersome machines, which overturned easily if they ran off the narrow roads. Of one thing we could be certain: As the machine left, the engineer would blow two mournful blasts on the whistle. In my childish fancy, I imagined it was saying, "Gooooood-byeeeeeee!" On a still evening, those steel wheels could be heard grating on the graveled lanes for a mile.

Threshing day was a visitors' day on farms then. Often city friends or relatives drove out with a fancy horse and shining buggy or carriage to spend the afternoon. Not long after arriving, they came out to view the threshing scene, and they always seemed to enjoy seeing it again.

Sometimes the visitors were members of the families who had grown up on the farms and moved to town, but always liked to come home on threshing day. The womenfolk helped in the kitchen, and the men might get a pitchfork and go to work pitching sheaves just to show that they hadn't forgotten how to help thresh.

There were always at least six days of threshing in our neighborhood, a day at each farm. Since we never threshed on the Sabbath and often lost another day or two to wet weather, we usually were more than a week getting the job done. We looked forward to threshing all summer long. But after six days of dust, sweat and tired bodies, we were all about as happy to hear the engine blow its farewell as we had been to hear it announce its arrival.

Threshing days are good to remember, and I am glad that after so many years I can remember them so well. They brought happy times that will come no more because threshing is no longer done as it was then. Today, one man with a small self-propelled custom combine can thresh more acres in two hours than our old steam thresher and 12 men could thresh in a long summer day. ❖

Did You Ever See An Ash Hopper?

By Ella Casey

When I was a child, my parents owned a 220-acre farm in the beautiful foothills of the Ozark Mountains in northwestern Arkansas. Only about one-third of their farm was cultivated; the rest was beautiful woodland. All kinds of oak trees and an abundance of hickory nut and black walnut trees were scattered throughout this woodland. These wonderful nut trees gave us children lots of fun going nutting every fall. We gathered enough nuts to last all winter. We cracked them on the hearth, and then sat around the big fire, picking out the nutmeats and eating them anytime we wanted.

But I started to tell you about our ash hopper. Papa always kept a good ash hopper for us to use to carry out the ashes from the big fireplaces in our front room and kitchen and from the big wood-burning kitchen range.

To build an ash hopper, Papa took the team and wagon and one or both of my older brothers and went into the woods where he cut down a tree of just the right size. Then he cut a 6-foot length from the bottom of the tree and hauled it up to the woodpile out back of the house. With his broadax, Papa hewed one side of the log to make it flat.

Then, with his foot adz, he began to dig a wide trench in the solid green log. He kept digging until the trench was about 8 inches wide and almost as deep. It was dug from near one end all the way through the other end.

Papa placed this log on some rocks so that it was level with the flat trough side up. He then stood a solid wall of boards on end in the trough, and leaned them out to rest on a pole that was suspended between forked posts about 3 feet from the trough. He placed a slat over each crack between the boards to keep ashes from slipping out.

After securely nailing the boards to these poles, Papa put boards up in each end. Now the ash hopper was ready to use, ready to collect all the household's ashes.

Papa put up two posts, one at each end, and laid a long pole on top of them. Over this he stretched a wagon sheet and tied it down securely so no rain could wet our ashes.

When the hopper was almost full of ashes, our fun began. We children carried buckets of water from the well and poured it into the hopper until the ashes were soggy wet and the lye started to drip into the big stone jar in the pit Papa had dug under the open end of the trough. Mama used this lye to make our soap.

Papa told us when to add water and how much just to keep the lye running good. Mama tested the lye in the jar by dropping an egg in it. If the egg floated, it was strong enough to make the soft soap.

Mama kept the lye dipped out of the big jar and filled quite a few half-gallon fruit jars. She stored these jars of lye on a shelf in the smokehouse until hog-butchering time, the first big killing frost in the fall, when the weather got cold.

Mama made a small barrel of soft soap and kept it right inside the smokehouse door. She hung a dipper gourd on a nail right over the soap barrel. On wash days we each filled a small bowl-shaped gourd with soap and set it on the bench by our tub with the rub board in it.

We poured a little of the soap on the soiled collar or cuffs of a shirt and then rubbed it on the good old washboard. It sure made Mama's white clothes dazzling white. All of our clothes had that clean, clean look.

Wish I could buy some soft soap now for shampoo. It was the best shampoo I ever used. Where did soft soap go? ❖

Making Hay

By George King

Driving across mid-America, I couldn't help but notice rolls and rolls of hay lying in the fields at random. Sometimes the farmer had piled them in one corner of his field.

Today's farmer uses a machine that cuts the hay, rolls it into a manageable bundle, then ties it with wire, all in one operation. I couldn't help but think about making hay back in the 1920s, when we did it differently. We probably had more fun doing it our way.

It was our custom at haying time for several farmers and their families to join forces and harvest the hay on all of their farms. It was a cooperative effort and a festive occasion. The family whose fields were being harvested provided dinner—the midday meal—for all hands. It was often served outdoors on long tables, and was a joyous, lusty, noisy, sweaty affair. We celebrated the harvest to excess, working hard and eating heartily.

The stacker had to put up with kidding about whether or not his haystack would withstand the test of time and not get tilted out of kilter before winter.

The mowing machine had two wheels, a gearbox and a long cutting blade that extended out to the right of the wheels. The machine required one driver and a team of horses to pull it. As the driver guided his team down the field in straight rows, the cutting blade mowed the hay, which remained on the ground.

After the mowing, a two-wheeled horse-drawn vehicle with a rake on the back gathered the hay off the ground and laid it out in rows. The farmers left the raked hay lying in the sun for a day or two to season. While one field of hay seasoned, they mowed another.

Returning to the field where the raked hay was waiting, men and boys used pitchforks to pile the hay into round shocks about 6 feet tall and 10 feet in diameter.

After shocking, the hay had to be stacked. They dragged the shocks to a predetermined location where two strong men with pitchforks pitched the hay to the stacker, who piled and arranged the hay into a large haystack.

Not uncommonly, all the hay in a field could be contained in one haystack. Come winter the farmer could take a ladder, climb to the top

of his stack, and pitch hay down to feed his cattle. If the stacker had done a good job back in haying season, the haystack repelled rainwater and was good for feeding, top to bottom.

Why did we have more fun at it in those days? Getting together was part of it. Also, occasional incidents provided fun and sometimes outright laughter. Take the time one of the older boys got a wasp in his overalls. He shed his overalls on the spot, ran and jumped into a nearby creek.

Dragging shocks to the haystack was fun.

The young people did this, using a horse or mule with harness and rope. They looped the rope around the shock at ground level, then clamped the free end at the singletree to complete the circle.

Once the hitch was complete one could drive the horse or mule and drag the shock to the haystack. Each driver had fun riding the shock, as he (or she, for sometimes the older girls took part in this) dragged it in.

A lot of joshing and daring took place at the haystack. The stacker had to put up with kidding about whether or not his haystack would withstand the test of time and not get tilted out of kilter before winter.

Often bets were made about it. The men who pitched hay from the shocks up to the stacker took dares as to how long they could go without a break. Much ado about showing strength and getting up a good sweat filled the scene.

The workers quaffed gallons of lemonade, made by the ladies. Young people got into contests of drinking spring water, probably not a healthful pursuit. But who thought about it in those days?

Snakes and other wildlife provided extra excitement. The mowing machine blade uncovered snakes and often cut off their heads as they lay coiled in presumed security. In those days the young people pounced on all snakes that survived the mowing blade and killed them. Some of them, such as copperheads, were poisonous.

Unfortunately, some birds' nests were suddenly brought to light and broken up as well. Quails' nests were the most commonly disturbed, and we definitely understood the old phrase, "scattered like quail."

Baby rabbits likewise ran desperately in all directions once the mowers disturbed their homes.

Sometimes the young people caught them and made pets of them, but often the family dogs got them. The dogs joined in the haying with gusto, joyously romping hither and thither.

We had a holiday, making hay. The weather was hot and sunny; we got tired and sweaty, but we just "let it all hang out!" I suppose the term "hayseed," referring to country folk, may have developed from hay-making, because we got hayseeds down our backs and in our shoes.

At the end of the working day the men and boys went down to the "ol' swimmin' hole," shed their clothes, and washed away the day's sweat and debris. It was an unforgettable time. ❖

The Fuel Supply

By Marie Freesmeyer

The source of our community's entire supply of fuel was the trees growing on ground that might, when cleared, be cultivated and made to produce, at least meagerly. Each year the farmers cleared portions of their hilly acreage so as to increase their tillable acres. Much of this newly cleared land in Calhoun County was rough and was usually later set out in apple trees.

This work of cutting trees, clearing the brush and undergrowth, and making the usable parts into wood for fuel was always done in winter. In fact, it was one of the principal jobs for that season, and required many hours of hard labor each day that the weather was "tolerable."

The tools consisted of a crosscut saw, several double-bitted axes and numerous wedges. Later, for splitting and sawing the wood into stove lengths, more axes and bucksaws were used. As far back as I can recall, though, the poles which were to be used for wood were stacked into huge piles to be sawed in one or two days by a traveling or custom-rigged circular saw powered by a steam engine, and later, a tractor. These stove lengths were then split or left whole for the heating stoves. Much of it had to be split fine for the cookstove. Of course, one soon became adept at recognizing pieces which would be difficult to split. These were thrown back to be used later for "heating wood."

Farm homes were usually quite large (so were the families), requiring several heaters that consumed an abundance of these large sticks by day and required several of the larger, tougher variety each night to hold fire ready for immediate heat the next morning. The faithful range in the kitchen ate a gigantic wood box of split wood each and every day except the hottest days of summer. Almost without exception, there were three meals to be cooked each day, to say nothing of the fuel required to heat wash water, bath water and irons, and to complete the canning, preserving, pickling and other chores, including heating the soldering iron, popping corn and toasting bread.

Town folks, too, needed nearly the same amount of fuel. To get their supply, they bargained with a farmer to haul them a certain number of cords. This "cordwood" was split portions of trunks or logs cut into 4-foot lengths. It was delivered and ranked on the purchaser's property for a sum agreed on beforehand. Sometimes the more industrious (or those less able to pay) made arrangements to cut the timber themselves in a nearby woodlot.

Cordwood had to be sawed into lengths suitable for the heaters by those who did such odd jobs about town. A sizable pile of cordwood could keep a man occupied for several days or even weeks, with only a sawbuck, a bucksaw and ax to work with. He probably did the job for a nominal price just to be occupied and to give him an opportunity to be among acquaintances so he could engage in lengthy conversations while resting. ❖

Where Our Timber Went

By Henry Bowman as told to Lois Costomiris

When I was a little boy, Dad went on a log rolling and said I could go along. I remember it so well.

At the turn of the century, every farm here in central Indiana had a great big woods on it. When I moved here 73 years ago when I was 18, the woods began up 80 rods north, plumb down to that back road, plumb up to my line here. Solid timber.

First thing, when a farmer decided he was going to clear off one of those woods for a field, he had to go through and deaden the timber. He'd take an ax and chop a ring around each tree; if you cut the bark clear through all around, no sap can go up and the tree will die. The farmer chopped into the tree a bit, too, about the height of a stump.

When the trees died, they'd either blow down or have to be cut down. Then there'd be clearings, as they were called. An old clearing is a sad thing to walk through—trees a-laying in every direction. It would be a very sad sight today, the way we need timber, but back then there was so much, and they needed the land to farm. Sometimes the clearing would catch fire in dry weather and burn over, but they paid no attention to that.

The men would cut a great big tree down, trim off the limbs, and pull it up to the great big crosscut saw. They set the tree on a big roller with huge spikes.

Several farmers gathered to prepare the trees for a log rolling. They'd take all the limbs off with axes and saws. Then it was ready for the log pile.

Then the day came when there was an announcement: "There's going to be a log rollin'!" All the men gathered to help and the women prepared dinner.

They used 6-foot wooden handspikes to carry the logs. Positioning the spikes under the big log all along it, one man carried from one side of the log and another man from the other side. In all it took a dozen or so men on each side to lift that awful weight.

Then the foreman yelled, "Lift!" Everybody started together. A lot of young fellas around 18, 19 and 20 years old were a-helping. It was natural for them to flex their muscles and try to outdo the others. They'd roll those logs way up into a high pile. The older men would help, but they weren't trying to outdo anyone else!

Then they'd set that afire. Biggest fire you ever did see. It would burn day and night for a week or more. Talk about smoke!

I was thinking the other day: If our forefathers had just had our modern chainsaws and the other big sawing equipment we have, how much easier it would have been for them.

You just don't realize the work it takes to make a clearing. How did they ever get it all cut down and piled and burned? The stumps had to be burned as best they could, but it took them a long, long time to rot so that they would burn completely. For a long time, they had to farm around stumps, gnarled, tangled roots and trash. It took years to make a really good field out of it—and to think the only tools they had were axes, handsaws and crosscut saws!

I'd go over and watch a neighbor, Calvin Tidler, saw logs with a big machine. He could hitch four or eight horses to it. Walking in a big circle, they provided the power, just like

for the old thrashing machines, and then he sawed the wood.

That old saw was a big, heavy thing. The horses would go around and it would saw away. It had a great big cogwheel to run the saw. Just look at the wood he could make!

The men would cut a great big tree down, trim off the limbs, and pull it up to the great big crosscut saw. They set the tree on a big roller with huge spikes, then started the team, and that old saw would start to buzzing. They could roll it, and as they rolled, the roller would pull it up another cut.

Calvin put his whole weight on that saw to hold it down. It threw out shavings in all directions. It was cut off a log, roll it up, cut off another log, all day long.

One day, George Williams—he was a loud talker—got the horses skeered, and one started to run off. He was a powerful big horse. He just tore that saw all to pieces. That ended the sawing.

Even with so much timber and so many leaves, I don't remember that there were any fires. When I was a kid, I never heard about wildfires like the ones they have out West now that tear through the timber.

This whole country was full of sawmills. They were run by steam, and they had boilers and engines. Near the mills stood tall piles of sawdust, waiting to rot down. It wasn't any good for anything after it rotted, not even manure. It turned black. I'll bet you a nickel you can plow through that spot today and see where the sawdust pile was; the soil will probably still be black.

People brought their logs to be sawed at these mills. Many built their buildings from timber off their own land. Every couple of miles there'd be a sawmill.

I can see those wagons yet, stacked high with what they called headin' blocks. They'd cut down a great big tree, bring a load of logs to the sawmill, saw the tree off in exact lengths, and then split each length into big chunks— headin' blocks. One of these would be all a person could lift. They'd have a rack made for the wagon, load it high with the headin' blocks, and then sell them to the old heading factory that made heads for barrels.

Wood was used for everything back then. It would be nice to have some of that fine timber back that went up in smoke in the old days. What would those old-timers think if they saw our countryside today, with no wood plots to speak of, and what trees there are, so old and diseased? ❖

The Farmer's Boy

The sun had set behind the hills,
Across the dreary moor,
When, weary and lame, a poor boy came
Up to a farmer's door.
"Can you tell me," said he, "if any there be
That will give me employ,
To plow and sow, reap and mow
And be a farmer's boy?

"My father is dead, and Mother is left
With her five children small,
And, what is worse for my mother still,
I'm the biggest of them all.
Though little I be, I fear no work,
If you will me employ,
To plow and sow, reap and mow
And be a farmer's boy.

"And if you will not me employ
One favor I will ask:
To shelter me till break of day
From this night's bitter blast.
And at break of day I'll trudge away
Elsewhere to seek employ,
To plow and sow, reap and mow
And be a farmer's boy."

The farmer's wife cried, "Try the lad,
Let him no further seek."
"Oh, yes, dear Father," the daughter cried,
While tears run down her cheek,
"For those that will work, it's hard to want
And wander for employ.
Don't turn him away, but let him stay
And be your farmer's boy."

In course of time he grew a man;
The good old farmer died
And left the lad the farm he had
And his daughter for his bride.
Now the lad a sturdy farmer is,
And oft he thinks with joy
On the lucky day he came that way
To be a farmer's boy.

John and Bill

By Wauketa Craw Wright

Our farm lay across a gentle slope that faced the Meridian Road. Mama had been a schoolteacher, and she told us it was the sixth principal meridian of the world. When we went to school they told us the same thing. It was in South Central Kansas, and when I was a youngster, it was a very pleasant place to live. We called the farm Old Sunny Slope. Cowskin Creek wandered along just north of it, and part of the tracks of the old Chisholm Trail crossed it broad pasture.

The house sat back from the road a ways, but those who passed could find us easily. Sometimes the gypsies camped along the creek bank, and would come asking for "a couple of chickens, "a basket of eggs" or "a side of bacon." Tramps would stop and enjoy a snack that Mama fixed for them as they sat on the well curb, and drank the cool water that the windmill pumped.

One early summer's day, John came up the farm lane. He was not a tramp, but at first sight he looked like one. He was short and ragged, with a shock of black hair and big dark eyes. He was dressed in dusty, rumpled clothes, and he spoke with a heavy accent. He said he was tired and hungry, but he wanted to work for anything he got.

Dad was coming up from the barn and met him. It was getting close to harvest time, and we would be needing extra help. Dad took him to the wash bench by the milkhouse, where there was a basin and soap, an old mirror and a towel. The farmhands cleaned up there before they came to the house.

John took off his coat and shook it, rolled up sleeves, and refreshed himself. Dad saw that

He deposited his money in Dad's name because he did not want to give his own full name. We never knew him by anything but "John."

he was a strong man, and he told him he could have a job through harvest, if he wanted it.

John slept that night on the back porch. The farmhouse had two screened porches, one on the front and one on the back. The front porch wrapped around three sides of the big east bedroom. These porches were our sleeping rooms through the hot summer months and our freezer in the winter. The hired men always slept on the back porch. It was on the west, and Dad had made a canvas curtain that could be rolled down as needed to keep out the hot afternoon sun or the rain. The back porch was also our laundry washroom. In the tubs, the hired men took their baths and washed their clothes.

John was wonderful help. He was steady, industrious and trustworthy. After he had been with us for several days he told Dad that he had some money with him, and asked if he could hide it. Around his waist he had a money belt with $500 in it. He wore it under his long johns. He wore this heavy underwear at all times, no matter how hot the weather.

Dad took him to town and introduced him to the banker. He had never been in a bank. He deposited his money in Dad's name because he did not want to give his own full name. We never knew him by anything but "John." Dad always paid him in cash, and we respected his secret.

He was good with the horses and all the animals on the farm. I had a Spitz pup that the keeper of the livery barn in Wichita had given me. The pup was so small that I carried it home in my coat pocket. John took a fancy to it, and named it Popo. He told us that he was Bohemian. One night, when we went to town to see a vaudeville show, John rocked Popo until we returned so he would not cry. He even helped me fix a doll cradle for Popo so I could rock him with my foot as I shelled peas or cut paper dolls.

We grew very fond of John and hated to see him go. He told us he spent his winters in Florida where he could lay on the sand and swim in the sea, and that he would be back again, come harvest time —and he was. For three years we had John each summer. During these visits he would tell us about his life as a boy in "the old country" and about his winters in

Florida. We watched for him to come back the fourth summer, but he never came. He had told us about a "pretty woman" who lived in the South, and said that someday he might want a home there. We often thought about John and wished him well.

Then, on another early summer's day, Bill came. He walked with a jaunty stride as he came up the farm lane. He was very different from John. He was tall and lean, young and handsome. He wore a belt and no suspenders, and a big hat cocked on a heady of heavy blond hair. His eyes were blue. He was also tired and hungry, and looking for work. His last name was no mystery. Right away he told us he was Bill Nickols, and he had come up from Texas.

He also proved to be strong, steady, industrious and trustworthy. He was also good with the animals, and even had an extra sense with horses. He seemed to speak their language, and they always worked well together.

Bill loved the prairie pasture, and taught us things about the wildflowers that we never knew. With his long pocketknife, he harvested the wild cactus that grew on the prairie, and sliced it for us to taste. He gathered the cactus blossoms that we

would never get close to because of the thorns.

We could hear him whistling wherever he went. He taught us his songs. There was, "Pony Boy, Pony Boy, won't you be my Pony Boy?" And then, "When you go back home to the girl that you love, remember little Mo-Hi in the coconut grove." I think I liked this one best: "Come take a ride in my flying machine, and visit the man in the moon."

He saddled Cricket, our graceful white mare, and taught my brother and me to saddle and ride her.

He helped repair the white picket gate to the farmyard. Mama always said, "The sun made it yellow all afternoon, and pink when the day is late." He told us stories of life on the Texas range, and helped us pick our strawberries and make ice cream. He even showed us how to fashion knickknacks out of leather and wood. He was almost like an older brother.

But one day, at the end of summer, he tossed his big hat onto the back of his head, gave us a jolly "So long," and went off down the farm lane.

Dad was very sorry to see him go. We all felt a little sad. We knew we would never see him again. ❖

Maple Sugaring

By Sarolin McVey Griggs

*S*ome of my earliest memories of growing up on our small, hilly farm in the late 1940s are of walking behind my dad through the woods, carrying a bucket of elder spiles, as he bored holes to tap the maple trees.

Late in January we cut elder branches about the circumference of a man's index finger. Sitting by the wood-burning cookstove in my mother's kitchen, Dad peeled off the bark and cut them into 5-inch lengths. He sharpened one end and reamed out the pithy core to make a channel for the sap to flow through.

I followed Dad through the woods with the bucket of spiles banging against my legs. I watched as he braced the hand drill against his chest and bored a hole deep into a maple tree. Wet, white spirals of wood followed the drill bit out of the hole. Then he drove an elder spile tightly into the tree with a mallet. Almost immediately the sap began to run through the channel and drop into the metal lard can we set under the spout.

The woods were muddy in the spring and the tractor mired down, so in the early years, we collected the sap into 10-gallon milk cans set on the back of a horse-drawn sled. The trees were widely scattered within an area a half-mile from the shed where the sap was boiled down.

The shed was a three-sided affair put together from scrap lumber and second-hand roofing. Two sides of it were support for the stacks of firewood that reached nearly to the top. Dad had cut wood from dead trees all winter to get enough to fuel the two 120-gallon pans in which the sap was reduced to maple syrup.

The warm, steamy shed was a cozy place in the cold early spring. Keeping the fire going required lots of wood and attention. Dad had an old long-handled corn popper that we stuck into the flames to make the best-tasting popcorn I've ever eaten.

Word spread among Dad's regular customers that the syrup was ready, and the cars then would start coming down our long, narrow lane, bringing people from town. They came to buy syrup, but they also came to walk across the footbridge to the sugar shed and see the boiling sap and talk

with Dad. My brother and I stayed close by but out of sight to watch and listen to these strangers who drove big cars and lived so differently in a town we rarely saw.

Mother sometimes let them peek into her cellar with its rows of canned vegetables and fruit, bins of potatoes and apples, and jars of honey and jam. Or she might take them to the henhouse to gather a few dozen eggs that were still warm. They'd look at the hams hanging from the smokehouse rafters or watch us milk our sturdy, gentle cows, and I thought they found us as strange and different as they seemed to us.

I know now that even as I envied them—their cars, their sophistication, their "town lives"— they envied the snug security of our family. And they envied the serenity and independence of my father, whose time clock was the sun and the seasons, and whose small world was very much in his control. ❖

Sorghum Making

By Elsie E. Smith

*I*n 1929, Dad decided to make sorghum on the family home place near Flora, Ill., just as his father had done. He bought a cane mill that sat on four posts. Its three rollers—one large one and two small ones—stood on end and fit together tightly so that when the cane was fed into it, all the juice was squeezed out.

Two horses powered the mill. They were hitched to a large sweep that was fastened to the large roller; gears turned the other two. Guided by a line, the horses moved in a circle all day, operating the rollers that squeezed the juice from the cane.

Then Dad built a brick furnace 4 feet wide by 15 feet long. At its front he used pieces of pipe for grates and dug a hole under them for an ash hole. There was a large door in front of the firebox. At the back of the furnace was a tall smokestack to draw the fire under the pan.

Next he made a copper pan to fit the furnace. It had a divider that kept the uncooked juice separated from the almost-done product. The front of the pan was slightly higher than the back so that the juice gradually cooked into sorghum on the way down.

The cane had to be grown first, though. When word went out that Dad would make sorghum that fall, most folks bought seed and planted some cane. Ten acres was the most we ever raised. It had to be hoed several times each summer, and that was a job for the whole family. In the fall, before the first frost, we began blading the cane (taking the leaves off). We used paddles specially made for stripping leaves, but some folks used their hands.

Next, the cane was cut and laid in straight piles. Then it was topped, and hauled into the cane yard. The tops were picked up later and used for chicken feed. In the cane yard, all around the mill, we had set posts in the ground and nailed two boards crisscrossed on top. We piled our cane on end around the posts. Neighbors hauled their cane into the yard, too. Timing was important; if cane froze, it was ruined.

We had a lot of wind and rain that fall and the cane blew down. It was very crooked. Some said it was "Hoover cane" because it was trying to make both ends meet.

When Dad decided to make sorghum we discovered how tough the job was— and how sweet the rewards would be.

My older sister, Mildred, carried the cane to a box by the mill and my brother, Victor, fed it into the mill. The juice ran out into a half-barrel, strained through a sack that removed the largest trash. Then the juice traveled through a pipe to a large settling tank downhill, running through another filter along the way. The juice settled in a tank until it was drained off.

The pressed cane stalks were hauled to a field and left to rot. By the next year it was rotten enough to make good covering for strawberries. We called it cane pomace, but the real name for it is bagasse.

I was only 10 that first year we made sorghum. My job was to let the raw juice into the front end of the pan and take off the first skimmings that rose to the top and collected at the sides when the juice started to boil. At the edges of the pan, the skimmings were very green; in the center, where the juice had cooked more, they were greenish yellow.

Dad took care of the back of the pan where the sorghum was finished. He could tell when it

was done by the way it boiled and dropped from his paddle. Usually the finished sorghum was golden yellow. Sometimes, when someone had raised cane on ground that was too rich, the sorghum was dark. When it was done, he drained it off into a cooling pan and shifted more juice down. When the cooling pan was full, or when we had finished processing one man's sorghum, we put it in containers.

It took about 6 gallons of juice to make 1 gallon of sorghum. Of course, if someone wanted real thick sorghum, they got less of it from their cane.

Sorghum making was one job that we had to do seven days a week. We had to cook all the juice that had been pressed each day. You could smell the steam from the boiling juice a long way off. When the fire was burning big, the steam rolled until we couldn't see from one end of the pan to the other. It really kept us on the jump, but it was a job I always liked.

People came from miles around to watch us make sorghum and to sample the foam from the cooling pan. We always kept an ample supply of spoons and saucers handy for that purpose. As many as 120 people were there on a Sunday.

One old man didn't raise any cane himself,

but every fall he walked about 6 miles to our cane yard, bringing his pint cup. He just had to have a drink of that raw cane juice, with its sweet, "greenish" taste.

Most of the kids who visited were taken to the cane pile where they broke off a joint of cane, peeled off the outside and chewed the juice out of the center.

When the last of the day's juice was boiling in the pan each night, Dad began to pull the fire. Using a shovel with a 10-foot handle, he piled the burning wood and hot coals in a pile away from the sorghum shed. This pile stayed red most of the night and had fire inside all the time. We always warned folks to stay away from it. One day a man who had unloaded his cane started to drive away, and drove his team over the pile of coals. One horse's feet were badly burned. It took a long time before they finally healed.

When the pan finally cooled down in the evening, it was time to close the shed and retire for the night. After a long day's work we were ready to rest.

We usually kept around 40 gallons of sorghum each year. During the winter we enjoyed the sweet payback for all that hard work: taffy-pull parties and lots of popcorn balls! ❖

King Huskers

By Clarice L. Moon

When we lived in Iowa in the 1930s, corn was king. At that time open-pollinated corn was grown in the state. My dad raised Reed's Yellow Dent, which grew so tall that it reached for the sky.

In the fall, after the first frost, Dad went out with a team and wagon to snap out the ear corn from the standing corn. It was hard work for a young girl—hard on my back, with so much stooping to get the ears when some of the cornstalks fell over.

When snapping out ear corn, we didn't have to be as careful to get all the husks off the ear. That corn was to be hog feed, and they could still get at the corn if the ears had a few husks left on them. But if you wanted clean ears of corn, they had to be husked clean right in the field. If they were to be sold or ground for cow feed, they had to be free from husks.

When snapping corn, as when husking corn, we wore a husking peg over our gloves. We could wear holes in our gloves in just one day.

At that time in Iowa, farmers didn't have many dairy cows, so as soon as a field of standing corn was picked free of corn, the feeder steers and pigs were turned into the field to "hog it off," meaning they could eat any ears left behind. But a farmer had to have good, hog-proof fences around any fields he was "hogging off"; if he didn't and his hogs got out, they would be found in the next county.

Hogs, with their "plowshare" snouts, gloried in digging in the dirt for things to eat. They could root under the tightest fence in seconds if not constantly watched, but who had the time? Still, neighbors took a dim view when 50 head of the neighbor's hogs made short work of their own unharvested cornfields, so the fences had to be "hog tight." My dad solved that problem by nailing several strands of barbwire at the bottom of the fencing. The sharp barbs discouraged hogs from rooting under the fence.

My dad had another trick up his sleeve: He put rings in their noses. He had a sort of pliers that held a ring as it was placed on the hog's snout and clamped down. It only took an instant to put them in after the pig was caught—but catching them was the rub.

Pigs can run like the wind. The only way to catch them was to herd a group into a building or a chute. Then two men went in among the hogs, one to hold each hog steady while the other quickly crimped a ring in its nose. Because it hurt to root in the dirt with rings in their snouts, the rings kept them from digging under fences.

The picked corn ended up in a bin heaped high with golden ears. Sometime during the winter my dad selected the seed corn for the next year's planting by choosing ears that were large and well filled to the ends with straight rows of well-shaped kernels.

I helped Dad rack up the seed corn to dry. He took two long lengths of binding twine and at the halfway point in each, made a loop around an ear of corn as a base. Then he crossed the twine around an ear of corn and laid another ear in the crossed twine. The twine was crossed over that ear of corn and so on until there was a long rack of ears. We made several of these racks of

> *I helped Dad rack up the seed corn to dry. He took two long lengths of binding twine and at the halfway point in each, made a loop around an ear of corn as a base.*

corn to dry for seed and hung them on a wall to keep the mice out.

Later, near spring, we ran the ears through the corn sheller. As I turned the handle, the shelled corn fell into a bucket underneath the sheller. The seed corn was poured into a gunnysack and stored until time for spring planting. We gathered up the corncobs and carried them to the house where they were used to start the morning fire in the kitchen range.

In those days, the corn planter was set up to run on a wire

stretched across the field. Knots in the wire tripped the corn planter to drop seeds at regular measured intervals from each other. This method of planting was called "checking corn," which meant that each corn seed was planted so that as it grew, it could be cultivated in both north-south and east-west directions. It was believed to result in a greater yield in weed-free fields.

The corn was cultivated five or six times during the summer before it grew too tall and broke off under the cultivator. Then it was "laid by" and allowed to grow on its own.

Corn liked a good rain and strong sun. When I stood in a field of corn, I could actually hear it squeak as it grew rapidly under the hot sun.

In those years, a farmer really took care of his corn with two-row and four-row cultivators pulled by teams of horses. When I was about 14 I had my own two-row cultivator and team. After breakfast I harnessed my team and hitched them up. My perch on the seat was something like riding on a sulky as they do in harness racing.

When I reached the cornfield, I turned the

horses onto the rows and rode up and down the field, digging into the black soil to kill the weeds, the little corn plants marching by in a row between the plowshares. My dad worked in the same field with his four-row cultivator. It was monotonous work for the horses and drivers. We were ready to knock off when the sun was overhead so the horses could have a drink and a feeding of oats and Dad and I could have the dinner that Mom had ready. I usually carried a jug of water into the field to drink when I was thirsty.

After dinner we were back in the field again, and when we had it plowed, we moved to another. When that one was finished, likely as not the hay was ready to be cut and I'd be out mowing down purple alfalfa and red clover. But getting in the hay was a whole new ballgame.

Handpicking corn has gone the way of the dodo, with machines doing so much of the work. But I will never forget when corn was king—grown and harvested by the raw power of man. ❖

"But a Woman's Work ..."

Chapter Two

Even though I learned all about a man's world of work on the farm with Daddy, I don't think I would have ever learned what hard work means without the guiding influence of three of the hardest working women I have ever known.

The first was my Grandma Stamps.

Grandma was widowed with three small children when my mother was just a baby. Grandpa Stamps was in his 30s when he and Grandma married. Ten years later, he came in from the fields complaining of a headache; he was dead and Grandma was in mourning within a couple of days.

In those days, there was no Social Security or welfare. A young widow of 30, could find another man to marry, but with three children not many men were interested in taking on that kind of responsibility. She could give up her children, but for Grandma that wasn't even an option. Or she could work hard.

Grandma worked hard. She had a small farm and she put it to the most productive use she could. She never drove a car, but she could step into the traces of a walking plow behind a couple of cantankerous mules and steer them wherever she wanted to go. Several years ago there was a popular song that extolled the virtues of modern woman: "I can bring home the bacon; fry it up in a pan." Well, Grandma raised the bacon, butchered the bacon and cured the bacon—all before she had the chance to get it in the skillet.

For all she did, she must have instilled a great sense of loyalty in her children. One of her sons remained a bachelor and cared for her until her death at age of 91. Mama and Daddy made their home only a quarter-mile from Grandma, and we three kids—her only grandchildren—were able to visit her every day of our growing-up years.

Mama also learned the meaning of working hard from her mother. Mama helped Daddy build the home that would be theirs for life. Through sweat, splinters, mashed fingers and sometimes mashed feelings they worked side-by-side as our home grew with the family.

Mama always said, "The Lord helps those who help themselves." She did all she could to help herself and her family. She was a seamstress, and took in sewing from all over the county to bolster Daddy's meager earnings from the farm and the lumber mill where he worked "on the side." From the pantry and fruit cellar came our winter's hot meals, all earned by the sweat of her brow in the summer. With Daddy working such long hours to make ends meet during those tough days.

Mama's influence in my own life could be summed up in the words of an old song: "I want a girl just like the girl who married dear old Dad." That girl was a fiery redhead named Janice. She was 16 when we met, 17 when I had the courage to ask her for a date and 18 when we married. Some might say she "only" has a high school education. I say she is one of the most educated women I have ever known.

Like Mama with Daddy, she helped me raise three children. She has been shoulder-to-shoulder with me, whether working the farm— or editing a book. Even though she doesn't have to, she likes to work in the garden. She still likes the taste of fresh green beans and tomatoes. Our old farmhouse isn't air-conditioned, but she puts off canner after canner of vegetables each summer. To say she "works like a man" would be an insult. She works like a woman.

I'm glad I had these three examples of working womanhood in my life. Grandma, Mama and my dear wife Janice taught me the absolute truth "A woman's work is never done ..."

—*Ken Tate*

A Farmer's Wife

By Virginia Sewell

Last spring, as I was driving on a four-lane highway near some big farms in Indiana, I came upon a huge green field disk. Each side folded up toward the center, making it small enough to transport on the highway. Unfolded, it could cut a 20-foot swath.

I thought of how farming has become a big industry. With the machines they have now, farmers can work as much as 220 acres, all from an air-conditioned cab. They can till more in half an hour than their grandfathers could in a long, sweat-stained, backbreaking day.

My mind flashed back to farming in the 1920s and '30s, when men farmed with horses and two-bottomed plows, then later with riding plows.

Women had their role in the hard work, too. My 93-year-old sister-in-law, Lela, who has lived on the farm all her life, remembers helping as a farmer's daughter and later, as a farmer's wife.

Up at dawn, the wife and daughters prepared a hearty breakfast of eggs, bacon, sausage or ham, fried potatoes, homemade biscuits and gravy, and steaming cups of coffee.

Spring brought planting the garden. After the man plowed the plot, the women raked the clods to a coarse, sandy consistency. The main crops were potatoes, Irish and sweet. The potatoes were cut in chunks, each with an eye. If there was no eye in it, it was put back for cooking.

Other crops were peas, beans, beets and cucumbers. Then came the backbreaking job of setting out tomatoes, cabbage and onions. Most homes had beautiful flowers, too, kept under the care of the women.

Another task was spring cleaning, a very tiring, but rewarding job. Curtains and drapes were taken down, washed and ironed. Windows were washed inside and out with a pitcher of vinegar and water. Then it was time to rehang the curtains and drapes.

Rugs were taken up, hung on the line and beaten with a carpet beater that resembled a tennis racquet. Mattresses were carried outside and cleaned, or new ones were made from straw or feathers. Pillows were made with feathers plucked from ducks or geese. This cleaning was repeated in the fall.

Summer brought hoeing and weeding in the garden. "We always wore sunbonnets in the summer to keep from getting sunburned or tanned," Lela said.

Lela recalled doing the laundry. Monday was laundry day. A fire was made outside under a large iron kettle to heat the water. "We gathered corncobs, sticks of wood or limbs to heat the water," she remembered. "We then scrubbed the clothes on a washboard in a galvanized tub. Another tub was used for rinsing the clothes. Mom made her own lye soap."

Years ago, wringing the clothes was done by hand, which was very hard on the wrists. The clothes were hung on the line, winter and summer. In winter, the clothes froze on the line, making it an icy chore to bring them in.

They were then hung on lines strung across the kitchen to finish drying. Clothes that needed ironing (before the days of permanent press and dryers), were sprinkled on Monday evening, then rolled up, placed in a basket, covered with a towel, and left ready to iron the next day.

Monday's menu was cornbread and beans with ham. This seemed to be the norm in every home. I guess it must have been because the beans and ham could simmer all day long by itself.

Dresses were sometimes made from printed feed sacks and bloomers from flour sacks.

Tuesday was ironing day. Irons were heated on the kitchen stove. Some irons had removable handles. Others didn't, so a hot pad was used on them. "We had some burned fingers," Lela said.

She recalled spreading a cloth on the table to use as an ironing board. Smiling, she said, "My sister, Inez, being the oldest, always got to iron first. She would pick out the easiest ones to iron, leaving the rest for Anna and me."

Mending was done—seams stitched, overalls patched (most men wore bib overalls), dresses and aprons repaired, and buttons replaced—on Tuesday, too.

Somehow women found time to make quilts and rag rugs. Mothers and big sisters made clothing for the family. Dresses were sometimes made from printed feed sacks and bloomers from flour sacks.

"Women made their own bread using homemade yeast," Lela said. "Mom made her own yeast using hops that vined along the garden fence. She would make three loaves at a time."

Fall brought canning of beans, corn, peas, pumpkins and berries. Sauerkraut and pickled beans were made in barrels.

Farmers butchered their own hogs and cattle; then the women set to work. They cooked the meat and used it to make souse or scrapple. Chunks of fat were rendered into lard and tallow.

At harvesting time, all the farmers took turns gathering at each other's farms. A farmer who owned a threshing machine would bring it in and thresh the crop while the other men raked, loaded and transported the grain to the barn.

Then they would move on to another farm. It was a neighborhood project, with the women gathering to cook big meals for the hungry men.

The farmer's wife and daughters had a lot of hard work, but it really didn't seem so stressful as they visited friends and neighbors, had picnics or went fishing or walking in the woods. They found time to read or do other hobbies, as did Lela, who painted beautiful landscapes, which now are displayed throughout her home. ❖

A Recipe for Lye Soap

Use 2 quarts of melted grease from bacon drippings or scraps of fat meat. Stir in 1 cup lye dissolved in 1 quart water. This will get hot during the mixing process.

Allow it to cool until lukewarm.

At once, add 1 cup ammonia and 2 tablespoons borax dissolved in ½ cup water. Stir for 5 minutes or until too stiff to handle.

Put away to harden. It is best to let it set for 4 weeks. Nearly all soaps are better when they get older.

One advantage over commercial soap is that the natural glycerine remains in the mixture. Also, it's cheaper.

Lela's Recipe for Scrapple

1½ pounds lean pork pieces
1½ cups yellow cornmeal
1½ teaspoons salt
1 cup cold water

Cook the pork in 2 quarts water until meat is tender. Cool the meat and remove the bones and fat. Chop the meat fine and refrigerate. Chill the broth.

Remove the hardened fat from the cold broth. Place 4 cups broth in a large saucepan and bring to a boil; add the chopped meat.

Mix the cornmeal, salt and 1 cup cold water and gradually add it to the boiling broth, stirring constantly until it thickens.

Reduce the heat to low and cover. Cook for 30 minutes. Stir occasionally, as it will stick easily to the pan.

Pour into an oiled 9 x 3-inch loaf pan, cover and refrigerate several hours or overnight. When very firm, cut into ½-inch slices. Flour the slices and brown on both sides in hot vegetable oil. Serve with warm maple syrup or pancake syrup.

Mama's Mama

Mama's mama, on a cold winter day,
Milked the cows, and fed them hay.
Slopped the hogs, saddled the mule,
And got her seven children off to school.
Did a washing, scrubbed the floors,
Washed the windows and did the chores.

Cooked a dish of home-dried fruit,
Pressed her husband's Sunday suit.
Swept the parlor and made her bed,
Baked a dozen loaves of bread.
Split some firewood, lugged it in,
Enough to fill the kitchen bin.

Cleaned the lamps, and put in oil,
Stewed some apples she thought might spoil,
Churned the butter, baked a cake,
Looked out, and said, "For mercy's sake,
The calves are out of their pen!"
Went out and put them in again.

Gathered the eggs and locked the stable,
Returned to the house and set the table,
Cooked a supper that was delicious,
Afterwards washed up all the dishes.
Fed the cats, sprinkled the clothes,
Mended a basket full of hose,
Then, opened the organ and began to play,
When You Come to the End of the Perfect Day.

— *Author Unknown*

Cookie Day

By Mayna Milstead

When I was a child, growing up on a farm in Missouri, one of my favorite days was Cookie Day. Saturday was Cookie Day. By Friday, Mother had done the family washing and ironing and everything had been mended and put neatly away. The house had been cleaned from top to bottom. The feather beds had been shook and aired and the beds had been made up with clean, fresh linens. The parlor had been dusted and swept, and the Franklin stove laid with kindling to be lit on Sunday morning. Everything was ready for cookie day.

Preparations for cookie day really began on Friday. After school, sister Mary and I took two pans to the woodshed to collect walnuts and hickory nuts that had been stored there for the winter. Mary cracked the walnuts while I cracked the hickory nuts. We were both very careful to hold them on their sides and hammer gently so that they would not scatter, and so the nut meats would come out easily and mostly whole.

After supper, the whole family gathered around the big dining-room table. Mother and we children picked out the nut meats while Father played the guitar and sang.

Mother was the first one up on Saturday morning, as she was every morning. It took a lot of courage on those winter mornings to crawl out from the warm feather bed and covers, knowing that the fire had probably burned out and the downstairs was practically as cold as the upstairs. But by the time the rest of us got up, the big kitchen was warm and cozy and the dining-room stove was going full blast.

It was not nearly so hard for us to get up on Saturday morning as it was through the week. There were always so many interesting things to do on Saturday. If we finished with all our chores by noon, we could go skating on the little creek or ride our sleds down the long hill behind the barn. Or, we might make a snowman and build a fort in the backyard, or follow all of the queer, interesting, little animal tracks that ran through the woods. There were always so many interesting things to do that we could never find time to do them all. And, of course, there was the wonderful fun of making cookies.

As soon as breakfast was over, everyone got busy. My

job was to clear away breakfast and do the dishes while Mary did the churning. She sat patiently on a kitchen stool and plunged the wooden dasher up and down in the earthen churn, making little splashing sounds. Sometimes it took a long time and the rest of us had to help her with the task.

Bill and John's main chore was filling the woodshed. Right after breakfast, they put the racks on their sleds and started making trips back and forth to the huge pile of sawed wood. By noon, they had the shed filled, the wood stacked neatly in cords against the wall. It was piled to the rafters—the green wood and dry wood on opposite sides, and the small cookstove wood and kindling placed within easy reach of the door.

The shed was connected to the house by a passageway. It always gave me a warm, comforting feeling to see the shed filled with wood. Let it snow and blow; nothing could keep us from being warm.

After the dishes and churning were done and Mother had finished making the beds, we started the cookies. Out came the mixing bowls, molasses, spices, brown sugar and white sugar, the raisins, plump and sweet, the nut meats, and all of the other ingredients we needed.

Mother mixed the batter while I rolled and cut and Mary took care of the baking. We always made several different kinds—oatmeal, chewy with nuts and raisins; molasses, with their never-to-be-forgotten flavor; gingersnaps and

cookie jars from the pantry shelf, the large brown one and the china one, decorated with kittens and daisies, that had a handle like a bucket.

While we filled the cookie jars, Mother cleaned the breadboard and brought the chilled pie dough from the window box. There would be pies for Sunday, too, two mince and two pumpkin. With the plump dressed hen hanging in the cellar house, the main part of Sunday dinner would be completed.

By 11 o'clock, the cookies were all done and stored away in the jars. The pies were cooling on the pantry shelf and the bread, crisp, fresh and fragrant, was in the warming oven. The big kitchen was cleaned, warm and cozy, filled with delicious aromas from the morning's baking.

After dinner, we hurried into our boots and heavy wraps, anxious to be outdoors and doing all of the things we planned. There would be no more cooking for the day. For supper we would have the rest of the roast, sliced cold for sandwiches, with crisp, spicy pickles and huge glasses of cold milk from the cellar house. There would be cookies and canned peaches with thick, heavy cream for dessert.

gingerbread boys, with raisin eyes, noses and mouths; and huge, crisp sugar cookies made with rich, fresh butter.

On the back of the stove, while the cookies were baking, a loin of pork simmered in the iron kettle. Later, potatoes, carrots and small, sweet onions would be added. In the oven, the brown pot of beans baked slowly, sending forth a delicious aroma of molasses, tomato sauce and spicy brown sugar every time we opened the door. On the warming oven, the loaves of bread Mother had made were beginning to rise above the pan. They would be put in in time to bake to a crisp golden brown. Dinner would be no problem, with the fresh churned butter, the rest of the spice cake left from the day before and canned blackberry sauce.

As Mary took the cookies from the oven, she stacked them in piles on the tray. When they had cooled, Mary and I got down the

Saturday afternoons passed quickly, and it was usually dusk before we trudged back up the hill behind the barn. The oil lamp in the window, lighting a path on the snow, was a welcome sight. Inside were warmth and comfort and love.

After supper was over and the Saturday night baths were out of the way, we all gathered in the dining room where we studied our Sunday school lessons and each of us read a verse from the Bible.

The day's activities, the fresh air, the hot baths and the warm fire made us all drowsy, and long before Father had finished reading the last chapter of Corinthians, we were all nodding.

Cookie day was over. It was time to get into our flannel nightclothes and race through the icy halls and up the stairs to be tucked and snuggled into the big, soft beds. ❖

Separating the Women From the Girls

By Annabelle Scott Whobrey

Today, farm wives go on diets, do exercise and take vitamins. Mercy! When I was a full-fledged farm wife, I'd never heard of such a way of life! I suppose I'd have been classed as a "free-lance health addict." Food and exercise went with the role of farm wife.

I had a perfect exercise machine: a cream separator. It wasn't exactly bought with my "figger" in mind, but I sure stayed slim and trim!

I wasn't as sold on the salesman's pitch as my husband was. It was an advancement in farming that nobody else in our neighborhood owned—or so the salesman said. All farmers had milk cows, and the cream was skimmed from the milk crocks by hand. This new contraption was supposed to pay for itself with the cream it saved. Looking back, I'd bet my bottom dollar that that salesman was a city slicker who didn't know cream from blue john. But he knew how to convince my husband that every good dairy farmer used a separator.

Without asking me, I was given the chore of operating and cleaning the thing. It didn't work nearly as easily as I was told it would. I had sore muscles to prove my point! After cleaning all those dozens of metal disks, I knew a cream separator was no prize. And all the water it took to clean the thing didn't come at the turn of a tap; I had to wrestle it from a contrary old pump on our back porch—another muscle-building chore that wasn't eliminated until electricity hit the farm front!

Getting the milk from the cows didn't always come easy, either. I knew it was the coldest job in winter and the hottest in summer. Learning to perch on a three-legged stool and hold the milk pail between my knees while working the ol' pull-and-tug was no breeze. Coping with a cow's tail full of cockleburs kept a milkmaid on her toes!

Don't get me wrong; there were a few moments of pure enchantment. Nothing soothed my nerves more than a leisurely walk after the cows in the evening. There abounded the birds, rabbits and wildflowers that no city sister ever encountered.

To say I never understood the workings of that cream separator is an understatement. To this day, I don't know how the cream came out one place and the milk another. But I had faith; I put the fresh milk into the 5-gallon container atop the separator and set the vessels on shelves to catch the results.

I saved some whole milk for the house and the skimmed milk went to the hog pen. Those swine thought the swill was delicious: milk mixed with shorts and leftovers from our kitchen. It helped fatten the hogs to be butchered just before Christmas.

Life on the farm has changed. Cream separators are now collector's items, sitting in yards with pots of posies on each shelf. I give thanks I no longer have to struggle with the "exercise machine." But looking in a full-length mirror, I realize I should! But return to the cream separator? No way—even though it sure was a way to tell the women from the girls! No wonder the younger generations would rather go to health spas! ❖

Frugal Flowers

By Nelle Portrey Davis

It was mid-February. A typical prairie blizzard was raging outside, but our little homestead cabin was snug and warm. The day before, father had made the weekly trip to town and picked up the mail. The Shumway Seed Catalog had finally arrived.

Mother was seated at the big dining table, making out the seed order. I, an eager 6-year-old, was beside her. Lettuce, pumpkins, cabbage, carrots, turnips—all the common, everyday vegetables were considered and choices made. I knew these must come first, but would Mother never turn to the pages of flowers? There were illustrations of so many, and I hoped she would order a package of seed for every one.

But money was scarce. There were many mouths to feed and Mother was frugal. When it came to the flower seed, she explained she was ordering a package of mixed flowers seeds. "The children's special," it was called, and was described as "a large package of mixed varieties of annuals." While most of the flower seeds were 5, 6 or 7 cents per package, this mixed package was but a penny when added to the regular order. As Mother explained it, it sounded like a wonderful bargain.

It was some weeks before the seeds arrived. I was eager to see the package of flower seeds. After supper was over and the dishes put away, Mother opened the plump package and emptied the seed onto a large white platter. Then I pressed close beside her as she carefully examined our treasure. My eyes mist as I think of this beauty-starved woman, shaking the seeds about, sorting and recognizing most of

them, and dreaming of the blossoms she hoped to enjoy during the summer. She had been raised in Wisconsin, where every rural home was graced with a profusion of summer flowers. The bleak, windswept prairies would seem more like home if she could have the brightness of summer blooms.

With little sauce dishes arranged around the platter, Mother set about sorting the seeds. There were a dozen or so of the big nasturtium seeds. They would be planted in a little bed by themselves, she explained as she sorted. The easily recognized four o'clocks came next. Then the morning glory seeds; she explained they would climb up beside the kitchen window. Dahlia seeds were segregated, too. Then, with a moistened toothpick, she picked out the little pointed pansy seeds. There were many of those. Marigold and zinnia seeds were picked out, too.

When the sorting was finished, there was about a teaspoon of small seeds left. Mother showed me in the catalog that these seeds were a mixture of poppies, petunias, asters, bachelor's buttons, calendulas and larkspur.

Again, I was beside Mother when the planting was done. First were the little flats for the dahlia and pansy seed. A pane of glass was laid over each flat until the seedlings appeared.

When the actual garden planting started, each variety of seed was planted in a different row, and all seeds were planted sparingly. "We don't want the plants so thick that we have to thin them out," Mother explained. The small, mixed seeds were covered with only a sifting of soil. Then gunnysacks were spread over the row. To keep the sacks moist, Mother punctured the bottom of a tomato can with many small nail holes; then, carrying a bucket of water down the row, she watered the rows with the can, using it as a sprinkler.

The flowers thrived and bloomed, and were enjoyed by the family and neighbors. By the time winter came, Mother had made many small envelopes and filled them with seeds she had saved from her flowers. In future years, if she could spare a few cents for flower seeds, she could purchase other varieties, for she already had seeds from her old standbys from her "penny package."

That is one of my favorite memories of my mother: the two of us on our knees, crawling down the row every morning as the annuals came up, Mother pointing out the various seedlings she remembered from her girlhood.

Later we moved to the Pacific Northwest, refugees from the Dust Bowl. We were very nearly broke, thanks to the Great Depression and the Dust Era. But now, at last, we were making a home where rainfall was plentiful, soil was good, and seasons mild. Now it would be possible to raise all the perennials and shrubs we wished, besides our annuals. Mother, well-versed in horticulture, assured me that most of perennials could be raised successfully from seed.

She chose a seed catalog from a firm that specialized in flowers. We could not afford to order as many as we wanted that first year, and besides, our ground needed much work before planting, for this was the cut-over stump land in northern Idaho. The plots where brushfires had left ashes were chosen for our first seed beds. We spaded the ground, sprinkled it with wood ashes to sweeten it, and raked it smooth.

The first year we could afford but three packages of perennial seeds: long-spurred columbine, digitalis (or foxglove) and delphinium (larkspur). The little seedlings grew beyond our wildest expectations. We really had more plants than we had bargained for, and we shared with neighbors who had never dreamed of raising their

bedding plants from seed. They had always bought flats of seedlings from the local nursery.

The next year, we had more plots ready for planting, and we managed to get a few more packages of seed. Gradually, year by year, our flower gardens expanded. How well I remember those spring and summer mornings, when I would see Mother leave her little cabin, coffee cup in hand, to visit the flower beds. She was eager to see the growth what had occurred since the previous day. I would join her, finishing my own cup of coffee, and we went from bed to bed, enjoying the beauty of the morning, the fresh mountain air and the song of birds as they flitted about.

I am not sure I remember all the perennial flowers we established. Besides those already mentioned, the list included monkshood, coreopsis, dahlias, pinks, sweet williams, gaillardia, cineraria, phlox, rudbeckia and shasta daisies. Every variety proved a success.

When autumn came, we were sorry to see our beauties succumb to colder weather. We each took up two or three of the bright cineraria for winter potted plants. We enjoyed them so much that we determined to try more seedlings for indoor pleasure the following winter.

We sent for angel rose seed, achimenes, browallia, impatiens and abutilon, starting them in flats set in sheltered spots in midsummer. In the fall, all were potted and brought indoors. Many found their way to neighboring homes, as our windows would not accommodate all. Remembering the pansies we had used for houseplants when I was a child, we lifted a couple of the choicest to set on a window ledge on the north side of the living room.

> *We sent for angel rose seed, achimenes, browallia, impatiens and abutilon, starting them in flats set in sheltered spots in midsummer.*

The potting soil was good, and we put gravel in the bottom of the pots for drainage. All went well until one morning, when we discovered that the beautifully blooming impatiens were covered with aphids. Nothing could be found on the other plants.

"This is a simple problem, and easily solved," Mother assured me. "We will just spray the plants with mild soapsuds. The soap will not hurt the plants, but it will get rid of the lice." Her remedy worked, and I have used it successfully for many years.

The achimenes were lovely little plants, growing and blooming well with very little sunshine. The little tubers, which looked like miniature pinecones, multiplied quickly and increased from year to year. The abutilon (flowering maple) grew so rankly that we had to pinch off the ends of the branches to control it. But it blossomed charmingly and lived for years (repotted occasionally), bringing pleasure to the family and providing a splendid conversation piece, as it was not commonly used as a potted plant.

Today, in every part of the country, the Latter-Day homesteaders are appearing. Most of them are seeking to create a home from scratch, with as little expense as possible. These people are learning that milk comes from cows, vegetables come from a home-tended garden, heat comes from wood, sweetening comes from bees, and clothes are sewed at home. So much for the creature comforts! But for "hyacinths to feed the soul"—blossoms and verdure to make the "homestead" a real home—I would advise the raising of perennial flowers from seed. The cost is extremely small, and the rewards enormous.

Last Sunday, an old friend, visiting her hometown for the first time in 35 years, asked me to accompany her on an afternoon drive "back in the boondocks where my grandparents homesteaded 70 years ago." We had trouble finding the place. "I don't see anything that looks familiar," she worried as we followed an old logging road, far from the paved highway.

Suddenly she brought the car to a stop. "Look! Look!" she exclaimed. "Grandma's lilacs!"

Grown up in a tangle of alder, dogwood and mountain ash, the white and lavender lilacs were trying valiantly to hold their own. We left the car and, pushing through the thorny brambles of wild blackberry bushes, we found the tumbledown chimney and the rotting logs that told us where the old homestead cabin had once stood. All about us, in the tangle of underbrush that screened the remnants of a home, were the surviving mementos of a pioneer woman who had loved beauty. Jonquils and narcissus had spread for rods beyond the homesite. It was certain the columbine, waving airily here and there, was not the native red variety.

"I remember!" my friend exclaimed. "Grandma's wild Colorado columbine! She raised them from seed she gathered when she was teaching school in Georgetown, Colo. How she loved them!"

Shasta daisies, sweet williams and perennial sweet peas grew there too, almost obliterated in the rank undergrowth. But they had survived, and my friend dug up clumps of these old-fashioned favorites to take back to her city home—irreplaceable heirlooms, very personal and very precious. ❖

Not in My Garden!

By Lucille Miller

As a small girl, I loved to help Mother in the garden. She taught me to distinguish the food and flower plants from the weeds, which we always threw into the hog pen. They would disappear until only the stiff stalks remained.

I knew that if we were to have a good garden, the weeds must go. We had pig parsley, ragweed, sorrel, nettles, thistles, wild morning glory, wild mustard and buckhorn. We always let a few milkweeds grow in back of the chicken pen for the monarch butterflies to lay their eggs on. And, of course, we battled dandelions (though we also ate the greens in early spring when they were tender). All kinds of grasses sneaked in whenever they could, too, like knotweed and nightshade.

I loved Queen Anne's lace, but still, it didn't belong in a vegetable garden! Neither did dock and wild tobacco plants. Then there was peppergrass. Sis and I loved to eat the spicy flowers. We used to make bird nests out of chickweed, wild buckwheat and cockleburs. We had millet, which wasn't a weed but grew wild, and lamb's lettuce, so green and perky. There was smartweed, like nettles, wild hops and lamb's quarters. And chicory, with the lovely blue flowers we hated to pull. At one time, pioneers cultivated it in gardens and used the ground dry roots as a coffee substitute.

Many weeds seem like plagues. Ragweed aggravates allergies in August and September, when it ripens. Canada thistle is such a nuisance that farmers are fined if they do not eliminate it. Yet, the weed produces a beautiful lavender flower; bees love them, and the thrushes love their seeds.

My father hated weeds. No matter how busy he was, he'd stop to pull one up. There is a satisfaction in yanking weeds and shaking the good dirt from their roots. Creeping cinquefoil and strawberry-leafed cinquefoil had beautiful, waxy yellow flowers. Goldenrod and purple wild asters brightened up roadsides in autumn.

Stinging nettle does just that. Brush against it or pull it, and your flesh stings and burns for hours. Purple tufted vetch (I call it wild alfalfa) was great chick food, and they loved sweet and red clover, too.

Bittersweet woody nightshade has pretty clusters of flowers on its vines that later turn to green, then red, berries. They seem to grow overnight. Yellow weasel snout grows along ditch banks. Marsh violets are also classified as weeds, but I call them wildflowers.

All weeds are in the scheme of life and have medicinal and practical uses. But they don't belong in my garden today—and Mother taught me that lesson those long years ago. ❖

When Mother Sheared Sheep

By Chris Jensen

ou? You can't shear sheep. You're a woman, and women can't shear sheep!" Mr. Rasmussen told Mother.

"Sure, I'm a woman," she answered, "and I certainly can shear sheep. I sheared many in the Old Country, and I'll shear your sheep for you!"

Mr. Rasmussen had just explained to Mother that he was going to visit his children in Salt Lake City. "I've got to go next Monday and this is Thursday. Those sheep of mine should have been sheared several weeks ago, but the regular shearers are out of town working and the rest don't know how. I could haul them to a shearing corral, but I just won't have time. The weather will be getting warmer and the sheep won't be able to stand it.

"What will people think of me that I have to ask a woman to shear my sheep?" Mr. Rasmussen said.

"I don't care what people think," answered my mother. "Nobody thought anything about it in Denmark, so why should they worry about it here?"

"Well, all right, if you're sure you can. You may keep the wool as payment for your services."

That evening, Mother and I walked over to Mr. Schultz's home. We had an old pair of shears I used for cutting weeds along the ditch bank, but Mother thought they were too old and rusty and had heard Will Schultz might have a newer pair. He used to shear sheep professionally. "Yes, I have a pair of shears," he said, "but what in the world do you need them for?"

"I'm going to shear Mr. Rasmussen's sheep," stated Mother.

"You? You're going to shear sheep? That's a man's job. It's hard work. No woman would have the strength."

"I've sheared plenty in the Old Country, and I'm going to shear these."

"Well, you are certainly welcome to use the shears," he said finally, "but I'd certainly like to see the results."

The following Monday, Mr. Rasmussen had already left when we got to his place. I pulled a small coaster wagon with burlap sacks in it for the clipped wool. Mother carried the shears. The handles were wrapped with heavy twine and the blades sparkled. She wore a long, heavy apron and a pair of Dad's big work shoes.

There were three sheep penned in a corner of Mr. Rasmussen's corral. Mother looked them over carefully. "Go get me a pitchfork," she commanded. "This place needs cleaning up before we start. You would never see a mess like this in the Old Country." She cleaned out the old straw right down to the dirt and had me carry over fresh straw until the sheep were walking in a clean pen.

I picked up a burlap sack and the two of us stepped into the pen. The sheep bunched into one corner, eyeing us nervously. They let out a few bleats, but Mother paid no attention. She grabbed one by a hind leg and soon had it on its back. It seemed like only a few seconds before she handed me a large wad of wool. The sheep protested once in a while, but she kept clipping with lightning speed.

Meanwhile, Will Schultz had come down and watched us over the corral fence. Then George Allread, came over from across the street. He left after a while, muttering something to Will that I couldn't hear. Then Will turned to

leave, saying, "Well, I'll be darned."

The wool almost filled three burlap bags. We loaded it onto the wagon and headed home. Mother looked tired, and she was drenched with perspiration. On the way home, we met P.D. Jensen, one of the town dignitaries. He had been mayor, and was principal of the high school. He had graduated from some Eastern university and spoke with an assumed English accent. "Good day, Mrs. Jensen," he said to my mother. "What are you hauling in those bags?"

"Wool," Mother answered.

"Wool? Where in the world did you get it?" he queried.

"Oh," Mother answered casually, "I sheared Mr. Rasmussen's three sheep."

"You? You sheared those sheep?"

Here we go again, I thought.

"That's unbelievable. Shearing is hard work for a man. I didn't think any woman would be strong enough to do it, let alone have the skill!"

"Well, I did it," she said.

After we got home, Mother dumped the wool in a huge heap on two old sheets on the summer-kitchen floor. "This is all we will do tonight," she said. "I've got to get the shears back to Will Schultz and come back and get supper ready."

Will Schultz was excited when we got to his place. "I've never seen anything like it! The way you handled those sheep and how fast and clean you were. I'd like to give you those shears as a present. I won't be using them again."

"No thanks," she said. "Those are probably the last sheep I will ever shear."

How We Made It in Arkansas

By Elizabeth Bowman Good

Irish potatoes dug from the ground,
Boiled and creamed or sliced
and browned;
Butter beans—the speckled kind—
Are those that first off come to mind.
Tomatoes—juicy, sweet and red;
Plump bell peppers and hot corn bread.
Fatback—if that's all we had,
Floured and fried, it wasn't bad!
Kentucky Wonders were favorite treats
Rubbing shoulders with pickled beets!
Buttered carrots and okra, fried;
Crisp green onions on the side;
Cabbage slaw and turnip greens;
Radishes, peas and pinto beans …
Buttermilk from the family cow …
"Dinner's 'most ready, so call 'em now.
Shoo the flies and shut the door.
We got enough! Don't need no more!"
Some words of thanks for all we had
Were offered by my preacher dad …
And then we ate—kids, Ma and Pa …
That's how we made it in Arkansas!

"You know," he went on, "you could make a lot of money as a professional sheep shearer. Matty," he said, turning to his wife, "you ought to see what she did. It's really amazing …" Then the two of them decided to walk back to our house with us. Matty was as excited as Will was.

I'm sure Mother did not anticipate the interest her wool clipping generated. Men and women came to see that pile of wool, commenting, "You? You clipped all that wool by yourself?"

For a time, it seemed there was dry and wet wool all over the summer kitchen, and a lot of it spilled over into our regular kitchen. Mother was going to use some of it to make a quilt. It was several weeks before we had piles and piles of clean, dry wool.

The wool was then carded, using rectangular wooden paddles with dozens of short wire bristles on one side; they looked like large, flat hairbrushes. We placed a handful of wool on the wires on one card paddle, then pulled the other over it, and worked the card paddles back and forth until we got a pad of finely combed wool. It seemed as if we made thousands of those pads.

One day after school, I came home to find a group of women sitting around a quilting frame in the bedroom. Four chairs had been placed so the backs held up the corners of the frame. Every other chair in the house was occupied by a woman working on Mother's new quilt. The wool pads had been placed evenly on a large piece of fabric, the bottom of the quilt. The top was a large piece of cloth with a star-shaped pattern. The women busily stitched along the patterns, all seeming to talk at once. I wondered how they could figure out who was talking to whom.

After two days, the quilt was finished. It was so beautiful that I thought Mother would use it immediately, but she folded it carefully and stowed it in a drawer. When certain friends came to see her, she would bring it out. Everyone commented on how beautiful the quilt was, but the most frequently heard comment was, "You? You sheared three sheep to get the wool for this?" ❖

When Women Worked in the Fields

By Kermit Holgren

In addition to all their other chores, farm women often helped with the field work. During haying time, they often drove a team on some haying machine. And at harvest, they usually helped shock grain.

It was hot, heavy work—and they dressed for it. Back in those days, it was a shame for a woman to be suntanned—"sunburned," they called it—so they wore clothes that covered them completely, including big straw hats to keep the sun off their faces. The sun brought out the freckles, and it took a lot of lemon juice to bleach them out.

There were no slacks or jeans made for women in those days, so they had to wear men's overalls and shirts. Men's clothes didn't fit women any better in those days than they do today, so all pretense of glamour and beauty was lost—or at least well concealed—under all the clothing. And to top it all, they slathered a thick layer of cold cream on their faces to keep their complexion from getting coarse or "outdoor appearing."

Most of them were ashamed to be seen in that get-up; they wouldn't be caught dead at a fire the way they looked! If strangers came around, the women did their best to stay out of sight.

And yet, the women did a lot of work that was supposed to be "man's work"—heavy, hot and hard. Many farmers, including myself, owe a lot to the women in our families for the help they gave when the work overwhelmed us. ❖

The Egg Woman

By Edna P. Bates

I grew up on a farm on the Niagara Peninsula. We grew fruit, so most of our income came only once a year, in the fall. This money had to pay for fertilizer, spray, machinery, baskets and the annual mortgage payment. To have a little money coming in for groceries and clothes the rest of the year, my father raised a few pigs, kept several cows and had a flock of hens.

For years, my mother made butter and sold it in the Hamilton market, 10 miles away. Each Saturday she left my two older sisters with her mother-in-law (I hadn't appeared yet!), loaded the butter and eggs into the buggy and drove down the steep road along the Niagara Escarpment. She "put up" the horse with a kindly farmer at the bottom of the "mountain" (as it is still called), and took her heavy baskets on the trolley that ran from Beamsville to Hamilton.

Many city ladies had a regular "butter-and-egg woman" and came each week to buy from her. Others liked to shop around. Equipped with a little spoon, they tasted different ladies' butter until they found some to their liking. They bought from her that week. The next week they went through the same process. This was part of their Saturday entertainment!

When her goods were sold, Mama did her shopping, then caught the trolley back at night, hitched her horse and drove back up the steep road, suffering from her usual Saturday "splitting" headache, to collect her children and go home.

Since we had no brothers, my sisters and I took over the farm jobs as soon as we were big enough. (No child labor laws then!) We picked fruit all summer and worked in the garden.

When I was still small, Mama quit making butter to sell, and we sold our cream to the creamery. Though we seldom went to the market anymore, we still had an egg route in the east end of Hamilton. By this time, our transportation was a Model-T Ford, the kind on which the driver pumped two pedals (I still don't know what they were!) to come up the mountain. If we were too low on gas to get up, the car could still make the grade—as long as we came up backwards!

Looking after the chickens was part of my life for as long as I can remember. We got the cute, fuzzy, yellow chicks when they were only a few days old. I had helped scour and disinfect the brooder house floor and put down clean shavings. Glass jars of clean water were turned upside down on pie plates so the water would seep out slowly as the chicks drank. Long metal feeders with round holes for their heads were supposed to keep them from wasting the expensive chicken mash and stop them from crowding each other. But being the silly creatures they are, nothing could stop them from that! Two always wanted to eat out of the same hole, and they would spend their time pecking and pushing each other instead of sensibly taking turns.

I had to enter the brooder house slowly and quietly, or every chick would run peeping madly into one corner. A few of the smaller ones would get smothered or trampled to death. And if the fire in the brooder stove went out at night, they would huddle in a big heap, and more would be dead by morning! It was a tricky business, raising chickens.

As soon as the little roosters began to grow tiny red combs, we could see the difference in their attitude toward life! Their squeaky little crows made them sound like boys whose voices were changing. Then my dad separated the sexes. The "cocks of the walk" were destined to be fattened and killed, but the pullets were kept to lay eggs, so they were fed differently. No use buying expensive "laying mash" for roosters who would never lay an egg to crow about!

I cleaned out the chicken house (a smelly job I still remember with no pleasure), fed and watered the chickens, and helped catch them when they had to be moved. That had to be done at night, by the light of a lantern before we had hydro in the chicken houses. The only time to catch chickens was while they slept. Otherwise they fled, crowing and cackling, while we chased them fruitlessly.

One winter our flock got a disease. Then I spent my evenings helping my dad dose them individually with "Somebody's Roup Cure" and wash out their pus-filled eyes and throats with purple potassium permanganate. That's another smell that lingers in my memory!

We gathered eggs frequently, as the hens broke them if we left them for long. We provided a whole row of cozy, straw-filled nests, but eight hens would still insist on laying in one nest, and fight for the chance to get in first. Other rugged individualists insisted on laying their eggs on the floor!

To be sure we got all the eggs each time, we

had to reach under every hen on the nest. Sometimes they resented this invasion of their privacy and viciously pecked the offending hand! Since I never knew which one would peck, I always poked my hand in quickly, hoping to take the hen by surprise. Sometimes I won, but more often, she did.

Hens have a vicious nature, anyway. Sometimes, for no apparent reason, several would chase one innocent victim and corner her. They'd start to peck her, and if once they drew blood, they would keep on till they tore her to pieces if no human was around to rescue her. (At times, I liken school kids to chickens: Once they find another child's "weak spot," they keep on till they tear him or her to pieces— emotionally, at least!)

We cleaned eggs and "candled" them, holding them in front of a bright light and looking to see if there were any blood spots in them. We graded them into different sizes using small "egg scales," and put brown ones in one basket, white ones in another. Then we were ready to take them on our Saturday egg route.

As soon as we were old enough to make change, we girls took turns going with my father on the egg route, relieving my mother of this weekly chore. As we knocked at each door, we would usually hear some child call, "Hey, Ma! Here's the egg woman!"

Our reception varied from house to house. Some housewives were up, dressed in neat cotton print, cheerful and bright. Others yawned their way to the door, wrapped in scruffy bathrobes and down-at-the-heel slippers. Some had a bowl ready with the change in it for us. Others kept us waiting while they hunted through the overflowing sink for a dish to put the eggs in and some money—or asked if they could pay next week. Some were friendly and chatty, others uncommunicative or complaining.

One bought only brown eggs, "because they have a richer flavor," while another would use only white ones, "because the brown eggs are too strong!" Actually, there is no difference—the insides taste the same, and who eats the shells? But the customer is always right, and woe betide us if we didn't have the right color! Leghorns laid white eggs and barred rocks brown ones. Fortunately, we had both for our particular customers. Each house had a smell as individual as the people who lived in it. I could have recognized each customer's house if I had gone in blindfolded!

Early in the fall, my father started to sell the broilers, the roosters that had been fattening on skim milk mixed with cornmeal. (Feeding them was another of my jobs. Trying to spread it in the wooden troughs while they greedily pushed and pecked had its problems, too. Little did they know that they were only hastening their own ends!) We took orders each week for these. Then we usually killed a few extra, as some ladies never knew a week ahead what they wanted! We killed them each Friday in the barn, and picking off the feathers was a chilly job in winter.

Our fryers were a beautiful golden yellow, with a delicious flavor. By Christmas, they would weigh 9 or 10 pounds—more like young turkeys than roosters! Our fryers bore no resemblance to the little 2- or 3-pound fryers sold in the supermarkets nowadays. "Suckling chickens," my father used to call them scornfully. The meat from his chickens had character!

Besides our eggs and chickens, we sold fruits in season, as well as some vegetables. We often grew green peas, yellow wax beans, scarlet tomatoes and new potatoes to take along. We had to pick them on Friday afternoons so they would be fresh.

Strawberries, raspberries, blackberries, cherries, plums, peaches, Bartlett pears, grapes and apples went along when their season came.

Some had a very limited sale, for most ladies bought just what they ate at the table. Very few of the more provident ones made jam or canned fruit for winter, as my mother always did.

We had apples from August till late winter: early Duchess, Wealthys, McIntosh Reds, Snowapples (always at Halloween time), Cortlands, Spys, Delicious and Jonathans. We carried two baskets of different kinds in one hand and the eggs in the other. Our apples were hand-polished and laid in two layers in 6-quart baskets. For the cynical housewife who thought the "junk" would be in the bottom layer, and that she would get more apples if they were piled in loosely and heaped up, we demonstrated: In an empty basket we laid our apples, to show her not only that the bottom ones were as nice as those on top, but that all the apples in our "packed" basket wouldn't fit in a loose basket! This demonstration invariably produced a sale.

One day, a lady came to the door, looked at my dad's apples, and without saying a word, just shook her head. "It's just as easy to nod it up and down," my resourceful dad said with a grin. She started to laugh—and ended up buying not one basket, but two!

As my sisters married and moved away, I went with my dad every week, so I began my own sideline. I made jam, jelly and relish in the summer and sold it during the winter. I also baked rolls, and chocolate squares and made doughnuts every Friday. This was my "pin money" during hard times. The prices were different then: One lady bought a 32-ounce jar of my grape jelly each week—for 35 cents!

My father is dead now, and I teach school. Government rules and regulations would prevent us from selling all these things door-to-door nowadays. We would have to get a vendor's license; our fruit would have to go through an inspection station, and health inspectors would check my kitchen. Such small individual enterprises as ours have gone by the board. But no doubt, some housewives still remember with some nostalgia the days when they heard that Saturday-morning call: "Hey, Ma! Here's the egg woman!" ❖

Making Butter

By Faye Miller

For many years, my mother and father had milk cows, probably half a dozen or more. They separated the milk with a cream separator. They put the milk through a strainer to remove the impurities, then turned a handle which gave power so that the cream came out one spout and the skim milk out the other. The skim milk was given to calves, pigs, cats and dogs. The cream was kept in crocks and my mother usually churned twice a week, on Wednesday and Saturday.

We had a barrel churn. My brother and I often took turns turning the churn. It sometimes took a long time; some days, it seemed to take forever. When it seemed as if it would never turn to butter, we often heard our mother chant, "Come, butter, come, Johnnie's standing at the gate, waiting for a butter cake. Come, butter, come." I don't know as it helped any, but I chanted the same thing.

When the butter finally arrived, Mom gathered it into a lump, put it in a big wooden butter bowl and then, with a wooden paddle whittled by my grandfather, she worked the buttermilk out of it. When all the buttermilk was worked out, the butter was put on a big steak platter and formed into a large loaf. Then Mom placed a large, wet butter towel on top.

Sometimes people bought a pound or so from her, but most of it went to the H.C. Fox Store in Coldwater, Ohio. That store sold groceries, hardware, clothing, shoes, sewing materials and everything else we needed.

Today, the store is gone—and so is that wonderful homemade butter. ❖

I Remember Turkeys

By Evelyn E. Amos

In the 1920s, almost everyone who lived in our little Idaho valley and the sagebrush foothills surrounding it raised a few turkeys to help pay the land taxes in the fall. As the men were busy with crops and livestock, it usually fell to the wives and children to manage the poultry.

I think my mother must have been a real turkey expert. In the fall, she picked 10–20 of the choicest young hens and a gobbler or two to hold over the winter for the spring breeding.

When the mud dried up and the weather grew warm, I would come home from the one-room school on the hill to find her out with saw and hammer, mending old coops and building new ones from scraps of lumber. Sometimes she would say, "See that hen over there? I think she has a nest. Would you follow her when I turn her out?"

Would I? Nothing was more fun when the grass was greening and the yellow violets in bloom than to slip through the brush under the willows and cottonwood trees playing turkey detective. Those hens had a hiding instinct. They wouldn't go directly to their nests if they suspected anyone was watching. Instead, they meandered along this way and that, completely off course, nonchalantly picking at the grass until they found a clump of bushes to hide behind. Then they ran like mad to get away from the spy, and disappeared like magic. Their bronzy-black feathers blended into the shadows as they settled down into their grassy nests, making it most difficult to find them.

If lucky enough to outwit the hen and find her nest, I left and returned later (after she had laid her eggs and rejoined the flock) to gather the accumulated eggs. I always left one for a nest egg, because if the nest was completely robbed, she would desert it. I carefully covered it with old leaves and grass (the way the hen had left it) to hide it from the searching eyes of marauders, especially the devilish magpies that would riddle the eggs with holes and eat part of the contents. The big speckled eggs were placed carefully in a box under my bed in the attic and turned every day, just as the hen would have done in her own nest.

When she stayed on her nest at twilight, it was a sure sign that she was through laying and ready to start setting. Then Mama would fix a nice straw nest in one of the little coops and place some of the precious eggs in it before slipping out in the early darkness to try to grab the hen by its legs before it jumped away. Sometimes the hens were real aggressive and protected their nests with wicked pecks. Mama wore long sleeves for protection, but even then, she always had black and blue spots on her arms during brooding season.

During brooding time, the gobblers spread their wings and tails and strutted around, gobbling noisily.

She carried the hen back to the prepared coop and gently shut it in. If the hen accepted the new nest, it took four weeks of setting before the eggs started to hatch. The date was always marked on the calendar. Every other day she had to be let out for food, water and exercise, then closely watched to see that she didn't let her eggs chill by staying off too long or return to her original wild nest.

During brooding time, the gobblers spread their wings and tails and strutted around, gobbling noisily. This wasn't so bad if they didn't get mean. But many were the times I watched in fear while Mama (less than 5 feet tall) warded off a gobbler with an old broom as he lunged at her with flopping wings and sharp, digging spurs. She didn't dare turn her back on him.

When the eggs started pipping and hatching, Mama would get down on her knees and reach under the hen to remove all empty shells that might slip over the ends of other eggs to prevent them from hatching. This was another hazardous task, as it meant more black and blue spots on her arms.

Sometimes unhatched eggs were broken and examined to see whether they were fertile, or why they didn't hatch. I found that job to be dangerous, too. One day I was all dressed up in my gingham best to go someplace, and Mama cracked an egg. It was rotten-rotten, and it exploded in my direction, all over my dress! I suppose there are not many odors worse than a really rotten egg!

A day or two after hatching, when the soft little downy babies were old enough to walk around, they and their mother hen were gathered up and taken to a larger coop bordered with a little runway pen where they could learn to eat and drink water from the upside-down glass jar fountains. At this time, each baby was marked with a round hole in the webbing of its left foot, made with a leather punch.

Mama soured great kettles of skim milk that had been run through the hand-cranked cream separator to the clabber stage, then made it into grainy cottage cheese on the old wood-burning kitchen range to feed to the tiny striped turkeys. Later in the summer, she let the milk set in barrels outside the barn until the hot sunshine turned the clabbered milk almost to cheese on top. Then she scooped if off and mixed it with ground grains, mostly bran and shorts. Her rough, work-worn right hand turned soft and lovely from mixing the feed. Whether the sour milk or the bran was the beauty ingredient, we never knew.

After the poults were large enough to be turned from the pens, it was a pleasure to watch them spreading out through the grass, learning to grab insects while they made contented little "Pert!" calls to keep them flocked together. When the hen, always on the alert for danger, turned her head up to one side, her piercing eye was watching a far-off hawk in the sky. If she decided there was immediate danger, she gave a special hawk warning—a quick, low, burring, "Pert!" as she squatted low in the grass. The little ones instantly hid in the undergrowth and lay still until they heard their mother's assuring "Pert!" that all was safe again.

Sudden thundershowers were a real threat. If the hen huddled down with the babies snuggled up safely under her feathers, all was well. But she seldom did this. Usually she started for home, with the babies following in the grass, their downy feathers soon soaking wet. We had to rush out into the fields in the downpour to hunt all over for the hens, who often hid in a dense growth of poison oak. Then we had to gather into baskets all the little ones we could locate by their mournful peeping, to keep them from chilling to death. Often we carried them to the kitchen and put them on the oven door to warm and dry.

In summer, after the young were old enough to range, they set up a loud "caulking" chorus at daybreak, and when turned from their pens at sunup, headed for the sagebrush hills at a run, leaving the creek-bottom land behind. Coyotes were always a risk. As we seldom had time to go along to protect the turkeys, they were on their own. When one of them discovered a snake, rattlesnake or otherwise, he sent out a loud, "Pert-pert!" and soon the whole flock was

gathered around in a "perting" circle as though charmed by the snake's head.

By the time the sun grew hot, their crops were rounded out, heavy with grasshoppers, and they would seek a drink from the mountain springs. Then they sat panting in the shade of thorn trees.

After the sun set behind the mountains, if they weren't home, we had to start up the dusty cow trail looking for them. Often, when they reached the edge of the mesa, they would lift their wings and jump off into a long homeward sail down into the fruit orchard. We had difficulty driving them home if night approached before we found them. They seemed to be almost blind in the twilight, and couldn't see where we wanted them to go.

Sometimes they really got the wanderlust and strayed off a mile or two farther to get mixed up with a neighbor's turkeys and start fighting.

Sometimes they really got the wanderlust and strayed off a mile or two farther to get mixed up with a neighbor's turkeys and start fighting. It was a tiring job, getting them separated and started home. Mama's brand, the hole in the foot, couldn't be seen without catching the turkey with a long wire hook for a close examination, but it was always sure proof if there was any doubt.

Domestic turkeys also have that wild instinct of wanting to roost high up in trees at night. Mama set pole roosts up in the pens, but covering them over the top with wire netting was too much for her. Sometimes great horned owls swooped down at night, scaring them. Then they would take to roosting in the thorn trees or on top of buildings.

We tried to keep them off the house at night, but it was almost impossible. Although we threw sticks and stones at them until they finally flew off, they came back as soon as we were out of sight. In the wintertime, tucked deep within my feather bed in the attic, I could still hear them shifting their weight on the shingles right over my head as they stood and turned in the snowy night. We could have clipped their large wings feathers to stop them from flying, but then they wouldn't have been able to get away from coyotes, bobcats and other animals.

The most embarrassing thing happened when I was old enough to have dates with the boys. I was scared to death that at night, just when we reached the steps, turkey droppings would roll down the roof and right onto our heads!

Skunks were another menace. Every now and then, we were wakened by the sickening sound of turkeys crashing into wire netting or flying over the house. "Oh, shaw," Mama would say as she and Papa rose to light the coal-oil lantern and go out to see what was wrong. The dogs were barking and dashing all around, but it was too dark and too late to find the skunk.

Turkeys were a nuisance, especially in the fall when they congregated near the feed troughs to fatten. If a stranger came, they gathered around and gobbled so loudly that no one could hear a word being said. Then, if he went into the house, they flew up onto his car and tromped around with dirty feet!

Papa laughed because I said I didn't like turkeys, "not even one little feather." This came about because at market time, before Thanksgiving, I would come home from school to find dead turkeys all around in the house—on tables, chairs and stands. Neighbors had come to help kill and pluck the turkeys, but they never bothered with the little black pinfeathers. Mama and the rest of us had to remove those in the warmth of the house.

Besides all the blood dripping from their heads onto newspapers and the nauseating smell of raw turkeys, we had to deal with those tiny feathers. Sometimes we pulled them out with pliers when our fingers grew too sore. As they dried, those tiny feathers fluffed up, and every whiff of stirring air sent them floating into every corner of the house. It took days to get them completely cleaned up. Hence, "not even one little feather."

The dressed turkeys were hung

to cool in the cellar, where it was hoped the cats couldn't reach high enough to eat their heads off. In the morning, they were loaded into the Model-T truck and hauled to town to meet the buyer. Some folks went with teams and wagons to wait in line well into the night, perhaps only to be disappointed by the small check they received. Lots of the turkeys were "docked" into lower-paying grades, as the buyer said they had crooked breast, broken wings, a bruise or tear in the skin, too many pinfeathers, or were underweight—perhaps half an ounce under the minimum for first class.

Prices had a way of quickly going down at market time. But as there were no other buyers offering a better price, the farmers had to accept what was offered, and just hope the next year would turn out better. Usually they made very little profit. But at least they always had turkey on the table at Thanksgiving—and the roaming turkeys kept the grasshoppers down so that poison insecticides weren't needed.

Yes, I remember turkeys! ❖

Wash Day on the Homestead

By Jean White

A family of six can soil a lot of clothing and bedding. Our family was no exception. However, our little mother, all 5 feet and 90 pounds of her, was equal to the task of keeping us clean.

Every Monday in the late 1920s and early 1930s, Mother got up an hour earlier than usual to get a roaring fire started in the old Home Comfort wood stove.

While it was getting hot, Mother sliced leftover potatoes to make hash browns for breakfast. We could always count on boiled potatoes for Sunday-night supper because the leftovers took very little time to prepare on Monday morning.

After breakfast, everyone carried water from the well about 100 yards from the house. It took several trips to get enough water to fill the copper wash boiler and rinse tub.

Cleanliness may be next to godliness, but it was also akin to lots of hard work!

Before the water reached the boiling point, Mother dipped out half of it into the zinc washtub, which she had placed on two wooden kitchen chairs facing each other. There was a corrugated metal washboard on one side of the tub and a hand-operated wringer on the other.

Into the remaining water, she mixed 2 tablespoons of Lewis lye along with a thinly sliced bar of P and G laundry soap. When the water, lye and soap came to a boil, it steamed the windows, and a caustic, pungent aroma filled the air.

Into this mixture went the white things. These were boiled for about 30 minutes. Mother lifted them from the boiler into the washtub with a "boiler stick," which was really a cutoff broomstick.

My little Mother stood behind the washboard, and as she worked, her dip-rub-scrub actually

became a tune. She worked steadily, pausing only to wring the scrubbed garment through the wringer. She always added a few drops of bluing to the rinse water to get the pure white that was not otherwise obtainable.

After all the laundry was wrung into the rinse water, Mother moved the wringer to the rinse tub. From there, each white garment was wrung again, this time into a wooden bushel basket.

Next, more water was carried in and the boiler was refilled to wash the colored things and overalls. The fire was stoked up again.

While the water heated, the tub was emptied and the whites were hung on the clothesline, making a row of dazzling white with splashes of color as more clothes were added. The sheets left a fragrance of purity as they rippled in the breeze.

Now the whole process was repeated, except that the colored things did not require boiling. After rinsing, however, the dresses and shirts had to be starched.

The starch was made by adding 2 tablespoons of Kingsford starch to cold water. The mixture was boiled until it made a thick, translucent paste. Into this, Mother dipped the clothes, then wrung them by hand. Now they were ready to hang.

Wash days of yesteryear left many treasured memories. As Mother was energetically scrubbing, she was no doubt dreaming of automatic washers and modern plumbing. ❖

Mama & Her Kitchen

By Carol Schneider

To enter that long-ago farm kitchen was to step into Mama's world—a world filled with hard work, talent and love. Bright papered walls, starched white curtains, yellow painted furniture and colorful braided rugs welcomed all to her kitchen. Organization was the key to Mama's success in maintaining a working kitchen.

Wash day fell on Monday. When the crackling and popping in the black wood stove turned into a steady roar, Mama knew the fire had reached the correct temperature. She wrestled the beat-up tin tub to the top of the hot stove. The hand pump squeaked and groaned when Mama worked the iron handle up and down, pumping buckets of cold water to fill the tub.

While the water heated, she tugged the wringer washer and square rinse tubs to the middle of the kitchen floor. Chug, chug, chanted the washing machine.

The strong odor of homemade lye soap filled the air. All the clean clothes hanging on the outdoor clothesline came from Mama's kitchen.

Each Tuesday, Mama ironed. She built a hot fire in the kitchen stove, regardless of the season. Mama used a removable handle to set metal irons onto the stove, first one and then another.

While the irons heated on the stove, Mama set a wooden ironing board in the middle of the kitchen floor. When the irons were hot, she again used the removable handle to pick up an iron. She ironed clothing until the iron began to cool, then repeated the process. By suppertime, the bushel basket of sprinkled clothing hung wrinkle-free in the closet.

On Wednesday, the treadle sewing machine took its place on the kitchen floor. Mama hummed softly with the radio while she constructed patterns, pinned, cut and sewed yards of material. The feel of crisp percale, the

rustle of taffeta and the luxury of velvet fired Mama's creative talents.

On Thursday, Mama placed the week's mending on the kitchen table. She darned worn socks, sewed on loose buttons and fixed torn seams.

Friday was special. On Friday, Mama baked. She set flour, yeast, sugar and spices on the kitchen table. She measured, stirred and mixed. Her family enjoyed the crunchy breads, two-crust pies, yeast rolls and yummy sugar cookies. Eating a piece of hot apple pie smothered in homemade ice cream was a family treat.

On Saturdays, the complete house received its weekly top-to-bottom cleaning.

Every Sunday, after church, Mama served a special dinner. Her lace tablecloth and blue-and-white china dishes gave the kitchen a festive air. Mama enjoyed the afternoon visiting with friends and family. Then on Monday, the routine began again.

At harvesttime, Mama's kitchen bustled with activity. She shelled peas, peeled peaches, chopped carrots and diced tomatoes. The flavor of the spicy, crisp pickles came from her secret recipe. She preserved, pickled, dried and bottled bushels of homegrown vegetables and fruit for her family to enjoy during the winter.

This old farm kitchen, with Mama at the hub, wrapped its loving arms around her family, molding and shaping their lives. ❖

An Explosive Memory

By Melody Miller

Everyone had an outhouse or "a little house out back" that served its purpose when nature called. This event took place on a small farm south of Edison, Neb., back in the early 1930s.

A farmer and his wife had a few acres of farmland. One day, the farmer's wife was cleaning some clothes with naphtha fluid. There were no dry-cleaning facilities then, so if a garment needed to be spotted or cleaned, it was washed in naphtha fluid and hung to dry. This fluid was also used in gas lanterns.

After cleaning a few garments, the farm wife wondered what to do with the fluid. Back then, if you didn't know what to do with such things, they were dumped down the outhouse hole—and this was exactly what she did with her bucket of naphtha fluid.

Soon after she poured the fluid down the outhouse hole, her husband came home and proceeded to the outhouse.

Now, there was one thing that the farmer enjoyed doing, and that was smoking his pipe while sitting on the throne in the outhouse. He took his pipe out of his pocket and carefully filled the bowl with tobacco.

He took a stick match from his overalls pocket, struck the match and lit the tobacco. Taking a few deep draws on the pipe to get his tobacco burning, he relaxed and thought about his accomplishments of the day—and then he dropped the match into the other hole of the outhouse.

Boom! The match, still lit, ignited the fumes and the naphtha fluid, and he got a flash burn on his posterior.

He ran out of the outhouse, hitching up his pants, and stood in amazement as the old outhouse burned to the ground.

After the farmer's posterior healed and a new outhouse was erected, there were plenty of laughs and jokes made about his experience. But it wasn't funny to the farmer at the time. ❖

Ma's Summer Kitchen

By Toni Novak

*I*t was 90 degrees outside when Ma was baking kolaches. The heat from the old black cookstove was stifling when Pa came in to dinner. "Must you bake on a hot day like this?" he asked.

"It's for the church doings tonight, don't you remember?" Ma said. Then she added, "If I only had a summer kitchen like Frannie's, the house wouldn't get so hot."

Pa made no comment, but as we sat down to dinner, I noticed his eyes often sought hers across the dinner table, as if he wanted to share his thoughts with her, but then decided to keep mum. Ma had often broached the subject of a summer kitchen, but her wish never materialized.

That fall, when harvest was over, Pa took a load of logs to the Deerbrook lumber mill and came back toward evening with a wagonload of lumber. He had a broad smile for Ma when she asked what he planned to do with it—and then we all knew Ma was going to get her summer kitchen.

It took him almost a month to build it. He had put in a chimney and two windows, and when it was finished he stood back and beamed, "There, now. Ma's got what she wanted!"

About a week later Ma had another surprise. When we saw Pa hitch the team up to the farm wagon, we thought he was going to town for supplies. Instead, he had gone to our little village freight depot, and came back with a huge crate on the back of the wagon. We all came out to see what it held, but Pa wasn't going to confide in us. All he said was, "Wait and see," in a mysterious sort of way. We knew it was Ma's birthday, but we couldn't imagine if this could be a gift, or something Pa needed for the farm.

Then he sent me over to the neighbor's house to ask the man to come help him unload the big crate. He drove the wagon right up to the back door. When the men opened the crate, a beautiful, gray enameled Kalamazoo cookstove was revealed. The men took our old black range outside and set the new one it its place while Ma just stood in wistful wonder, looking at it. "Happy birthday," Pa finally said, as Ma went into his arms. Our old black cookstove was then moved into the summer kitchen, where it served for many years.

Now, I must tell you of the many uses we had for this little building. It stood only about 10 feet from the main building, conveniently saving many steps.

In the spring, Ma moved her washtubs out there to do the weekly wash. She rubbed the clothes by hand on the washboard, using homemade soap. The white clothes had to be boiled in the copper boiler, where Ma had cut shavings of Fels Naphtha soap. They then had to be taken out with a "wash stick" and rinsed in two waters. Now we didn't have all the steam in our house.

This summer kitchen was also used as a nesting place for our brood hens. Ma fixed up two or three potato crates with straw to make nests for them. She put about 15 eggs under each setting hen, then a container of grain and one of water in each

corner of the crate, and put a second crate over the top. This assured each cluck her own privacy, as neither could disturb the other's nest.

There was no electricity on farms then, so we didn't have a bathroom, but we moved an over-sized washtub out there for our baths. Now we could enjoy more privacy while bathing.

In the fall, we didn't get the house all messed up when we made sauerkraut. No more mess, and no more kraut odors in our living quarters.

Later, during mushroom season, Ma dried bushels of mushrooms there, and during apple harvest we peeled, sliced and dried apples.

In winter, that summer kitchen made a good walk-in freezer. Ma had learned to can some meat after butchering, but she could also store some fresh meat, soup bones and sausages out there. It all kept very well during our cold Wisconsin winters.

Ma's summer kitchen was a dream come true, and she always said this was the best investment for the comfort of the busy farm wife.

Almost 70 years have passed. Ma and Pa are gone. The summer kitchen has begun to lean, and I noticed that I, too, have begun to bend. As we sometimes drive past what used to be our farm home, I get a little sentimental and say to myself, "We are growing old together." ❖

Black Cast-Iron Pot

By K. Cardell Thompson

I'll never forget the large, black, cast-iron pot that sat near the back door of our little farmhouse. Most women in our small farming community had one of those black stalwarts, standing like a sentinel in their backyard.

Not only did the ladies boil their clothes in them and get a very clean wash; the old pot served many other useful purposes.

Besides boiling clothes in it, my mom used it to render lard at hog-killing time in the fall. We trimmed the fat from the hog, chopped it into small squares and placed the fat in the pot. Then we added enough water to keep the fat from sticking. We kept a wood fire going near the bottom of the pot so the fat would melt, and stirred it constantly so the lard would be light and fluffy.

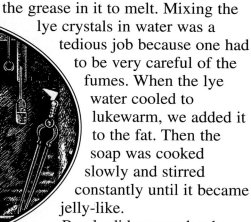

Eventually the water would evaporate and the "cracklings" would sink to the bottom. (Many ladies, including my mom, kept the cracklings to use when making bread.) We dipped the hot melted lard out of the pot and strained it into 1-gallon buckets, then stored them in a cool place to use during the winter.

One day at our one-room elementary school, some of the mothers got together and decided to make a large pot of vegetable soup for the children. They cooked it in a large, black, cast-iron pot.

As the soup bubbled over a wood fire, a delicious aroma permeated our classroom, making it difficult to concentrate on our studies. This was during the Depression, and many of us had little to eat at home. The soup was a special treat for our hungry little stomachs.

That might well have been the most delicious soup I have ever eaten, and, as I recall, I had my soup bowl filled more than once. The crackers served with the soup were nothing special, but to us they were the best crackers ever made.

My mother also used her iron pot to make lye soap. She saved bacon fat and other pork grease. We built a fire under the pot and placed the grease in it to melt. Mixing the lye crystals in water was a tedious job because one had to be very careful of the fumes. When the lye water cooled to lukewarm, we added it to the fat. Then the soap was cooked slowly and stirred constantly until it became jelly-like.

Rarely did my mother have borax or ammonia, but many ladies added these slowly to the mixture until it became thick, like honey. I heard that a few added some type of fragrance to their soap.

The mixture was poured into molds and cut into bars after 6–8 hours. It was left to dry, then stored in boxes. Mice and rats seem to like the soap, so beware if you ever make it.

We used this recipe, which was handed down from one generation to another:

5 pounds clean grease
1 can lye dissolved in 1 quart cold water
½ cup ammonia
¼ cup borax dissolved in 1 cup water
Special Note: The fumes from mixing lye and water can be dangerous, so be very careful. ❖

Life on the Prairie

By Grace La Rose

The year was a bountiful one for Midwestern farmers growing wheat, oats and barley, so my husband purchased a threshing rig with a large steam engine, a separator or thresher, and a mobile cooking/dining car which was towed behind the tractor as the rig move from farm to farm.

The cook, usually the wife of one of the crewmen, prepared meals from scratch for the 30-odd hungry workers. Breakfast, usually served from 5–6 a.m., consisted of pancakes, fried eggs, potatoes, bacon, biscuits, gravy, fresh fruit and plenty of coffee. Ham, turkey and beef sandwiches loaded the table for snacks at 10 a.m., followed by a heavy dinner at noon, an afternoon sandwich snack at 3 p.m., and finally a light supper at 7 p.m. Cakes and pies were always available.

The cook's helper was responsible for building the wood fire in the range, peeling potatoes, gathering fresh fruit, vegetables and milk, and helping with the dirty dishes, pans and kettles.

The 1924 threshing season began in early August. Late that month, the cook and her husband, the separator engineer, suddenly walked off the job. My husband replaced the engineer and hired me, a 23-year-old mother of a 4-year-old son, to become the cook for the next two months.

Life in the cook car left much to be desired, with only a few hours sleep, between 10 p.m. and 3 a.m. I slept on a cot at one end of the car.

I was on my feet all day, bending over a hot stove and washing dishes, clothes, etc. I can even recall many times standing on top of the stove, holding on to the shaky stovepipe as we rambled over the rough country roads or across fields to a new location.

The high point of the season occurred one noon when all hands were eating a hearty meal. I looked out just in time to see a roaring fire next to the separator. The straw pile had ignited, probably from tractor sparks blown by the strong wind, and the whole rig was about to go up in flames.

My shouts brought my husband running to the tractor, and he was able to pull the separator through the flames to safety with only minor damage. For a day or so, I was a true heroine, especially in the eyes of my husband.

At the end of the 1924 season, one forever etched in my memory, the $60 I received for my labors was all spent on a few pieces of badly needed furniture for our small rented house in Williston, N.D. ❖

Water Woes

By Louise Mattax

Now, Christine, I want you to steady the barrel and, Louise, you help her," Mama said. One of my earliest recollections is of Mama putting barrels in the wagon bed and hitching the team to go to Four Mile Creek after water.

The little farm Daddy bought in Oklahoma after he was injured in a train wreck didn't have a well. Daddy had been digging for one off and on when he was home, but just now he was off down around Tulsa with his threshing rig and crew—and we were out of water.

So Mama had hitched up Dan and Que, and was trying to load four oak barrels into the wagon. Christine was 10 and I was 6, so we couldn't help as much as we wanted, but finally the barrels were in and we set out for the creek about 3 miles from our house.

Mama drove along the rutted road, the barrels jiggling, while Christine and I attempted to keep them steady. Rhuhama, the baby sister, was only 3 and sat by Mama in the wagon seat.

It seemed like a long, hot trip that morning, but we made it to the creek. Mama drove the team into the creek until the wagon bed was almost even with the water. Then we began to dip with buckets—I used one that had held syrup—and soon the barrels were full.

With a lot of urging and slapping of lines, Dan and Que finally got the wagon up to the road. I was a tired little girl when we got home, but I helped unload the water into the barrels waiting on the back porch. It took a lot of effort not to go head over teakettle while trying to get as much water out as possible.

After we drained the barrels, Mama set two tubs of water in the sun for our evening baths. We soaped in one tub and rinsed in the other. Mama saved the rinse water to start the wash the next morning. The creek water was for baths, washing and the stock to drink. For drinking and cooking water, we walked a quarter of a mile to the neighbor's, who had a well.

The Chucklates were Cherokee Indian, and good neighbors. We would all take an evening walk up to their place and bring back water. When the white freestone peaches and the strawberries were bearing, Mama often took some along to give to them.

Daddy had never farmed, but was determined to make a go of it, so he had planted a little orchard and started a dairy herd by sending off for a Guernsey bull and two heifers. How we prized those cattle and their calves! Daddy would give us girls the calves, and if it was a bull calf, pay us 15–25 cents for the calf when it was taken away.

I never saw a well-digging rig when I was growing up. Everyone I knew hand-dug their wells, and that's what Daddy was doing. He had already tried three likely looking places, but had not yet hit water.

Then a friend told us of a water witcher who lived in a nearby town. Daddy wrote to him and the man came out a few days later. He took a branch off a peach tree and began to walk over the backyard. When the branch tipped to the ground, he told Daddy to try that spot.

When he had dug down several feet, he built a windlass over the top of the hole with a rope and bucket so that Mama could pull up the dirt, then send the bucket back down to be filled again. As Daddy dug deeper, he shored up the sides of the well with flat stones to keep the walls from collapsing, and so the water would not be muddy as it ran it.

Happy day! Daddy's efforts finally paid off, for he hit a good stream of water, cold and pure. Now we didn't have to hoard water! And no more trips to Four Mile Creek with the barrels! But we still walked over to the Chucklates for a visit and to take fruit from the orchard.

And you know, it seems like yesterday. ❖

Making Apple Cider

By Helen Colwell Oakley

*M*aking apple cider was exciting when I was a youngster in the 1930s, living with my family on a farm in New York state. As soon as the nights grew cold and frosty, thoughts turned to apple cider time.

The barn and farmhouse were a beehive of activity. Mom and Dad, the hired men, my brothers, sisters and I all scurried around the farm, searching for burlap bags, crates, jugs, bottles and a keg or two. We planned to make lots of cider this particular year, as there was a very good crop of apples, and besides, Halloween was just around the corner. A Halloween party wasn't an honest-to-goodness Halloween party without good old-fashioned sweet apple cider. Of course, it was even better if it had been made from our very own apple crop.

My younger brothers, Joe and Jim, bundled up in long underwear, overalls, flannel shirts, heavy plaid mackinaws, buckle boots and hats with ear flappers, and caught a ride with the horses and wagon heading for the apple orchard. (My brothers were around the ages of 8 and 10; I was perhaps 13 or 14. We had a houseful of children; besides my brothers, there were my sisters, six girls in all.) Later on—usually in late afternoon, when things had slowed down in the farmhouse—my sisters and I rode up on the wagon to help pick apples.

When we finally had enough crates and bags filled with apples, Dad loaded the farm truck up, and we were off to the cider mill.

The apple orchard was in back of the farmhouse, on a side hill. What fun it was to ride in a horse and wagon in those days. The hired man would holler, "Whoa!" and the horse would wait for us to load the crates and burlap bags of apples onto the wagon. Then he'd hoot, "Giddap!" and the horse would move on to another spot where the picking was better. We girls picked up the apples on the ground, but my brothers shimmied up the trees to shake the branches so that more apples would topple to the ground. If there were any bright, rosy red, luscious apples still clinging to the trees, the boys would gently drop them to us.

The choice apples were saved to use during the winter. Stored in the fruit cellar, they often lasted on into spring. Our potatoes were stored in a large wooden bin and the apples were right along side in another bin. We girls didn't enjoy making trips into the fruit cellar to fill a large pan

one away in a hurry. Then our brothers teased us about being scared of an itty-bitty worm; they weren't scared of worms—or much of anything.

When we finally had enough crates and bags filled with apples, Dad loaded the farm truck up and we were off to the cider mill in Hawleyton, a short distance from our farm. All of us children watched as the cider man washed the apples. Then he and Dad emptied them into the cider press. As the boards pressed down on the apples, out came the cider, squirting and oozing in every direction. Soon puddles of cider gathered in the troughs underneath, and the cider streamed into one of the large barrels we had brought. When that was full, the cider man filled our other barrels and several jugs.

Dad and my brother leaned over and got a drink of cider as it was

with potatoes or apples for paring; it was dark and kinda scary. We lost no time in filling our pan and getting out of there and back up to the country kitchen and pantry, where it was bright and cozy.

While we were gathering the apples at harvesttime, we sampled one every now and then. They were, beyond a doubt, the best I ever tasted, or so I thought—so juicy and sweet! Once in a while, when we came upon a fat worm wiggling down into an apple, we would toss that

just about through running. There was a tiny stream, and then just a drip or two before it finally stopped altogether.

The cider man was real busy, because most every farmer and neighbor with an apple tree or orchard was anxious to have some apple cider made before he closed down the press for the season. The cider man gave all of us girls samples of the cider in small paper cups. It was yummy, so cool and frothy and sweet!

Later on, after chores that night, Mom treated

us to freshly baked sugar cookies and glasses of sweet apple cider. We children didn't want to drink very much as we wanted to save it for the Halloween doings that would be coming up soon, but Mom assured us that there would be plenty to go around, "So drink up."

As did some of the other children at the Halloween parties, we brought a gallon of sweet apple cider. It sure was tasty with sugar doughnuts, plain doughnuts, raised doughnuts and cinnamon doughnuts, made by the mothers and big sisters. The treats were delightfully fresh and tasty, so they never lasted very long. My mom made doughnuts and then shook them in a brown paper bag until they were coated with powdered sugar. The time to eat them was right then, as they were best while they were still warm and moist.

At the grown-up doings for Halloween, the refreshments included all the sweet apple cider you could hold, along with trays of doughnuts and pies (usually apple and pumpkin) sliced into wedges.

In those days, there were always several Halloween parties going on in the neighborhood on the same night. The church halls, the granges, the schoolhouses and many of the houses, especially those with children, came to life around Halloween time with lighted pumpkins, sweet cider and doughnuts, and masked strangers making their way around the neighborhood on foot to trick-or-treat.

Besides the cider for Halloween parties, several jugs of cider were kept for cider vinegar to make pickles and use in other canning. And almost every farm cellar had a barrel or two of cider setting on the cellar bottom that would eventually work and turn into hard cider. Dad treated his friends to tall glasses of cider topped with eggnog. Mom wouldn't allow the youngsters to have any because it had "worked" and wasn't sweet. But Dad and the fellows seemed to enjoy the cider, as he refilled the glasses quite often.

Hard cider was quite popular with the gents, but the ladies wanted them to drink it sparingly. Apparently a little wasn't too bad, but if anyone overdid, it could be. One time the hired man loosened up the plug on Dad's barrel of hard cider. Apparently, he sampled too much of it as

he was repairing the potato bin, because he passed out on the cellar floor.

Mom wasn't too keen on keeping a barrel of hard cider around. But Dad was the life of the party when he served pitchers of cool hard cider to the crew as they were threshing oats, filling the silo or mowing hay. "Nothing like a long sip of cider to quench the thirst," he always said.

And, nothing like those cider-making days to make the Good Old Days on the farm even better. ❖

Reap the Harvest

By Beulah Alger Hoake

I remember pickin' apples,
Pickin' grapes, and makin' wine,
Huskin' corn, and haulin' pumpkins,
Rich and golden, from the vine.

Apple cider—apple butter,
Apples candied on a stick,
Halloween, and scary witches,
With their little bags of tricks.

I remember cellars groanin'
With the harvest all in tow,
Pickle barrels, and oh! my goodness!
Fruit jars stashed in a row …

On the shelves, all filled to brimmin' …
Peaches, pears and cherries red,
Snappin' beans and ripe tomatoes,
Turnip greens, and, golly Ned …

What a marvelous way of livin'
When the goodness of the land
Reaps for us a mighty bounty,
Just the way the Lord had planned.

Children's Chores

We were never bored back in the Good Old Days! There were always plenty of children's chores to keep us Tate youngsters occupied, both mind and body. If there was any time left over after chores, we learned quickly to busy ourselves with school work or just good, clean fun—or we might find ourselves recipients of more chores to fill up the time.

Summer or winter, fall or spring, the ritual was the same. Taking care of the stock meant slopping the hogs, graining the cattle and feeding the chickens. My older brother Dennis accompanied Daddy to milk the cattle while little sister Donna and I gathered eggs. Our workhorses had to be fed and watered in anticipation of the day's labors.

Donna helped Mama in the kitchen, while I more often than not found myself busy hoeing and weeding the garden.

I reveled in the pursuit of manly work, and looked forward to the time when Daddy would get around to letting me milk with him and my brother. Later, when I sprouted enough in my father's eyes to let me try out the milking stool and stall, I found it not all it was cracked up to be. That was particularly true when freezing temperatures and an unheated barn meant frigid fingers and a fidgety bovine that was probably as uncomfortable with the situation as I.

But it didn't matter how hard the work with Daddy was, it was much better than being relegated to "sissy" work with Mama and Donna. I helped with laundry, at least until Mama rolled my fingers into the wringer on the old washer when we were moving clothes from the washtub to the rinse tub. To my satisfaction, she always carried just a little guilt and didn't ask me to help with that again. Still, there was sweeping, cleaning and (horrors!) mopping.

One popular way Mama had to settle domestic disputes between my sister and me was to assign us to the same sink. I was the washer; she the rinser and dryer. The lesson in familial détente usually started with us not talking to each other. Then Donna usually broke the ice.

"You didn't get the gravy skillet clean," she said.

"Just rinse it off," I countered.

"That's not my job!"

"Is so!"

"Is not!"

"So!"

"Not!"

"Mama!" (usually chorused in unison).

But Mama made us work out our differences over that sink full of plates and flatware.

It was later in life that I discovered a valuable lesson. Mama and Daddy never used children's chores as punishment. Chores were opportunities for growth. They were a way to share the burden of making a living during tough times. They were a way to help a struggling farm family build a bond that would stand the test of time and adversity.

And as a side benefit, I was never bored.

Those chores helped me appreciate the times at twilight when the work was all done. I could watch the stars pop out from behind a velvet sky, listen to the katydids and the call of the whippoorwills, satisfied that I had done my part to help my parents and siblings. I could drink in the moment of having absolutely nothing to do with a pleasure the equal of which I have not felt since.

Working on the farm was a serious business for mothers and fathers as they strove to keep their families' collective heads above water. But, at the same time, we kids of the cornfield and chicken coop learned valuable life lessons from all those children's chores.

—Ken Tate

Rise & Shine

By W.F. Harvey

The night was cold, but I lay in bed warm and snug, wrapped in the quilt that Ma made. I was awakened with a start as the quilt was pulled from my body. There stood Pa. "Time to get up and do your chores."

"Aw, Pa. It ain't even light yet. Let me sleep at least until the sun comes up." I grabbed the quilt.

Pa pulled the quilt farther away and I fell out of bed. "Now that you're out of bed, get dressed. You'll just have time to milk your cow before breakfast."

I can remember how proud I was when Pa gave that calf to me. I was about 10 years old then. I didn't understand what Pa meant when he told Ma that it was time that I learn about responsibility. Responsibility was a snap. All I had to do was watch the calf grow!

That lasted for a whole week. Then Pa said that it was time to wean the calf. "Build a pen and keep the calf away from its mother," Pa said.

"But the calf still needs milk," I objected.

"It'll get milk morning and night, after we skim the cream off." Well, Pa didn't raise a completely stupid kid. I knew that this meant more work for me. Pa could call it responsibility, but I called it work.

I grabbed my milk bucket and ran outside. I could barely make out the outline of the barn in the morning's first light.

That night I learned that responsibility had another meaning. Pa showed me how to skim the cream from the milk and put it in the butter churn. Then he showed me how to heat the milk to just the right temperature.

"Now take it out and feed your calf," Pa said. "You might have to show it how to drink."

I went to the pen and set the bucket of milk down. The calf came to me but would have nothing to do with the bucket. I even knelt and pushed the calf's nose down into the milk. All that happened was that I got a face full of milk when the calf pulled its head out of the bucket and snorted in my face.

I heard Pa laugh as I wiped my face on my sleeve. "Son, the only way that a calf knows how to eat is to suck. Put your fingers in its mouth and stick its head in the bucket."

I did as I was told, and sure enough the calf started drinking. All went well until the bucket went nearly dry. Then the calf butted. I

thought that my hand was broken when it struck the opposite side of the bucket. The calf's teeth skinned the back of my fingers. Now I knew that responsibility also meant pain.

Three years later the calf grew into a cow and had a calf of its own. My chores grew to include milking. All of this went through my mind as I hurriedly threw my clothes on. I rushed downstairs and into the kitchen. Ma had a fire in the wood range.

"Gotta hurry," I told her as I grabbed my milk bucket and ran outside.

I could barely make out the outline of the barn in the morning's first light. The cold spring air bit my cheeks. I turned up my jacket collar to keep the chilly air from my ears.

I could hear Pa in the barn. I knew that Pa had already filled the manger with alfalfa hay. He was probably milking the first of his two cows.

I went into the barn where I found my milk stool by the light from a kerosene lantern hanging from a nail driven into a rafter. I didn't waste a movement as I slid into position to milk. I tried to get a head start on the challenge that I knew was coming from Pa.

"Last one done has to fill the wood box tonight," Pa said as he hung the full bucket on a peg driven into the post at the end of the stall.

I had already started milking by the time Pa sat down to his second cow. I had a steady rhythm going as milk struck the bottom of the bucket. Pa tried to increase his speed, but I matched him stroke for stroke. The milk in the buckets began to foam. All at once my cow went dry. I gave it a few stripping strokes to get the last few drops.

"I'm done," I said as I put up my stool. I felt generous, having won the contest. "I'll even carry your extra bucket to the house."

I was eating breakfast when Pa came in. Pa had a sheepish grin on his face. I couldn't hold back a beaming smile.

Ma wasn't one to take advantage of a situation, but she had to needle Pa a little.

"Jake, in honor of Waco wining the milking contest, I think that it would be nice if we sat around the heating stove in the living room tonight."

Pa gave me a proud look and said, "I'll make sure that both wood boxes are filled." ❖

Farmyard Treasure Hunt

By Doris Brecka

When I was a child, I thought farm folks had little kids around because they needed somebody to gather eggs. I could hardly imagine a farm without the challenge of hunting for hens' nests. Since we had no wire enclosure where hens could be let out for sunshine, Mama let them have the run of the place. She said they were healthier and lived longer if they could get out, pick at the green grass, and eat bugs and tiny pebbles. She must have been right because they laid a lot of eggs when they could be out.

In our flocks of chickens there was always the "establishment": a group of hens that continued to lay in the double row of nests against the wall. Usually by late afternoon, those nests did not contain many hens, except for a late layer or a hen that was becoming "broody" and wanted to sit on eggs to hatch them. Then I would have to reach my small hand carefully under her. Sometimes her response was a warning "Rrrr." But other times, I was treated to a quick peck on top of my hand, sometimes hard enough to break the skin or inflict a black-and-blue mark. The next time I would use a more cautious approach, poking a stick under the hen first. She'd promptly bite at it, and then I'd reach under her with my other hand to successfully extricate the egg.

Saturday was town day, when the sturdy egg basket full of spotless eggs was hoisted onto the front seat of the 1920 Dodge touring car.

Hens sometimes laid their eggs under the roost. Being short, I could get under the roost and search the corners to find the eggs before they got too old. Adjacent outbuildings were searched, especially if the "take" in the henhouse seemed smaller than normal. I looked carefully behind the doors, down into barrels, in bushel baskets and boxes.

A favorite place—and one almost inaccessible to grown-ups—was the machine shed. Hens often "stole" nests there, making a hollow in the cool dirt in the very farthest corners, usually behind the disk with its sharp round blades or under the tines of the spring-tooth harrow. I'd crawl carefully over these. Their very favorite spot seemed to be the old surrey. The wheels had been removed to retard decay and the main part was suspended from the rafters. I had to climb up the wheels of the grain drill to the top box, then over to the running board of the venerable old vehicle. Hens sometimes chose to lay on the ripped fabric of the front or

backseats. Their preferred spots, though, were under the seats. A flap of heavy greenish-black fabric completely hid the compartment, making it an ideal spot for a hen to seclude herself. In fact, this hideout might have gone without discovery had not a proud hen foolishly publicized her successful accomplishment with repeated raucous cackling.

The cool, dark cow barn was a favorite with hens, too. The cattle were out for the summer, but remnants of hay remained in corners of mangers, and the floors of the calf pens were still littered with straw. These made popular nesting spots. Occasionally, an adventurous hen threw caution to the wind and laid her egg up on a narrow stone ledge where there was no bedding at all. More than once, I discovered an egg that had rolled precipitously close to the edge.

The hay barn was another fascinating place to search. There were huge mountains of loose-harvested hay on either side of the inside driveway. Occasionally a nest would be at the very top. Sometimes I stopped to play with new kittens that I discovered curled up with their mother, deep in a cozy nest of hay. Mama always urged me to hurry, since it usually was nearing suppertime, so I hastened down again, happy to have added several more eggs to those in my half-gallon syrup pail.

True, I loved hunting eggs, but there were a few places that I didn't like to visit, including the spaces under the granary and under the porch. By the time I reached the nests in the farthest corners, I was almost shinnying on my stomach. Mama told me not to bother, but pride in my job wouldn't permit me to quit.

Most difficult to find were the nests that the hens often built in the long weeds and orchard grasses. There again, only the hen's cackling would give her away. If I discovered a nest with a lot of eggs, it would be "broken up" and the eggs all were thrown away. Or, if the hen seemed intent on keeping her nest, Mama would remove the eggs a few at a time and "candle" them, holding them up to a lamp to see if they were dark and thus might hatch. A hen sometimes hatched out 12 or 13 chicks.

Each day's "treasure hunt" was fun, but an additional reward was still to come. Saturday was town day, when the sturdy egg basket full of spotless eggs was hoisted onto the front seat of the 1920 Dodge touring car. I clambered happily up the running board into the huge backseat and, with Dad at the wheel, we took off, clouds of dust rolling up from our wheels. Traveling sedately at 30 miles per hour, the 3 miles to town seemed to take forever. But at last we parked near the tree-shaded courthouse just across from our favorite grocery store.

In the store, the eggs were counted by the grocer and Mama's supplies—mainly essentials like sugar, yeast, salt and cocoa, with occasional splurges of "boughten" cookies, bananas or canned pineapple—filled the basket again. Any surplus money was returned to her.

Having waited patiently for my nickel, I now flew next-door to the variety store with its long candy counter. I had to decide between half a bag of salted peanuts, a lunch-size bag of peanut-butter kisses, chocolate stars or pastel coconut bonbons. I might even think of the lean days ahead and select some hard candy—butterscotch dollars, striped peppermints or lemon drops. Another time it would be a candy bar; my favorites were Pieface and Fat Emma.

It was a wonderful lesson in economics that involved no charge cards, no checks—just a product we exchanged for things we needed and could not raise ourselves. I was proud to be a small part of it all. ❖

Stone Harvest

By Jack M. Harmon

Each year after the fields had been plowed and disked for the first time, it was time for the most unproductive harvest of all. We came to call it "the stone harvest."

My sister was drafted to drive the tractor pulling a stone boat up and down the fields very slowly. My brother and I walked beside it, picking up stones and tossing them onto the boat. When we came to one too big to lift, she would pull the stone boat alongside it and we would roll it aboard.

When we got a full load, it was dragged down to the hollow where we dumped them along the bank. The pile of stones got larger every year, yet, come spring, they were back on the fields. I often wondered where they all came from. Ma used to say that the Lord must have really loved flies, stones and poor people; that was why he made so many of them.

After a day of picking stones, my back was sore from all the bending and lifting. At least one of my fingers had been smashed, and the rest felt like they had been through a corn sheller. By the third day, my back had settled down to a dull ache and my fingers had acquired the texture of scabby sandpaper.

Those darn rocks were cold—colder than a landlord's heart at the end of the month. The air and ground could be warm—in fact it might even be hot enough to work in shirtsleeves—but those stones always had the cold, clammy feel of a grave. Seems funny; some folks believed the stones were lost souls the devil had rejected and sent back as a warning to the rest of us.

Oddly enough, if you farmed on shares, the landlord never wanted his share of the stone harvest. Owning our own farm, we were always thinking up ways to use the stones we had to pick up. But nothing ever came of these ideas, as any use we could think of involved handling them again. No way!

Mother insisted we pick some of the "nicer ones" for borders around walks and her flower beds. This was a miserable job. Before they could be set in place, they all had to be washed and whitewashed.

Someone in the past had had much more ambition than we had. The foundation under the house and barn had been laid up out of fieldstone. The springhouse and milk house were completely built from the stones, and even the well was lined with them.

As a boy, I always loved winter and hated to see spring come. I knew that right behind the birds and buds came the stone harvest, and all the other chores designed to make a boy's life a misery.

After considerable thought, I have come to the conclusion that the stone harvest was the most miserable job on a hill farm. But as I look back, it too is one of many things I miss from my boyhood.

The farm is gone now. Like many others, it has been subdivided into a community of homes. When I drive by it, I can't help wondering if the builders found as many fieldstones as my brother, sister and I did.

Although the farm was on a hill and the stone harvest was an annual chore, the farm provided a good living for the family. Even in those Depression times it provided plenty to eat and enough wood to warm us during the long, cold winters.

Yes, I miss the farm, Ma and Pa, and my brother who moved West and my sister who now lives in town. I don't suppose the stone harvest can be classified as part of the Good Old Days, but maybe it wasn't quite as bad as it seemed at the time. Time marches on and each step I take seems to take me closer to the past. ❖

To Market With Papa

By Esther Norman

When Papa attended the sale of his father's farm in 1917, he hadn't the slightest idea he was going to end up buying it. There were 10 children in his family, and it should have been bought by one of them, but Papa's excitement that day was too much. Mama's brother stood beside him and urged him to bid on it. Carried away, he bid once too often and the farm was sold to him.

Mama wept day and night for a week, saying she would never, never move to the farm. We lived in a house in the city. We had the conveniences of electricity, gas and water. A milkman brought our milk and an iceman brought our ice. Mama did her duty, though, and moved to the country. I remember wondering why she cried so hard after the furniture was deposited in our house in the country.

"Your brother Edward should have had this farm," my mother kept telling Papa. "How could you let my brother influence you to keep bidding?" Then she would cry some more. Papa tried to comfort her, but when he filled and lit the kerosene lamps, she cried some more. "Oh, my beautiful electric lights in town!" she wept. "How can I ever stand it?" Then she got ahold of herself and went to the kitchen and cooked supper on the big wood range. Papa had to keep putting wood into it.

We finally were settled, and the spring work began. Papa was a "market gardener," and that meant growing everything to eat, such as onions, green beans, lima beans, potatoes, tomatoes, sweet potatoes, carrots, cantaloupes, watermelons and other foods. It was hard work.

Papa planted seed onions, which meant much more work than just putting onion sets in the ground. But they grew to monstrous size, and they brought a big price.

He taught me to hoe correctly since he had grown up on a farm. "Gently," he would say, in his kindly manner, "loosen the loam up to a fine crumble. Be careful not to disturb the roots of anything. Be sure to pull all weeds carefully."

Well, seed onions are so delicate that it meant stooping down or creeping along on one's knees to get every little weed out. I grew to detest those onions, but they brought a good price.

Papa was good and proud of the fine green beans, and got $3 a bushel for them. It was about 1917–1918 and a war was on.

We had to be very careful about the tomatoes, too, as the vines could break easily. It was wonderful to see the huge, red, delicious tomatoes in rows about a block long.

I loved hoeing the cantaloupes and watermelons. I had to lift the vines carefully and hoe under them, then lay them back. I loved to see cucumbers and eggplant, so purple and shiny, growing in rows.

Every other day, Papa went to market. It had happened that our brand-new car was stolen just before we moved to the farm, so there was no transportation except to hitch up the horses, Blaze and Maude, to pull the market wagon to

town, about 7 miles away. That meant getting up at about 3 a.m. in the pitch dark and eating breakfast, then starting on the lonely road to town. I begged to go to market so much that they finally allowed me to go several times. I sat on the spring seat, jiggling up and down, and Papa drove. The loaded wagon had been packed the night before with baskets of beans, peas, tomatoes, potatoes, cucumbers, and sometimes plums and blackberries that grew wild. I will never forget those dark roads!

It was almost daylight by the time we reached the outskirts of St. Joseph, Mo. We passed the country club, and were able to go a lot faster on the paved road. As we went down Saint Joe Ave., Papa would stop at some of the grocery stores. The owners would come out and perhaps buy a bushel of beans or other produce. But I could hardly wait to get to Market Square.

It was a building about a block long, and on all four sides were stalls. Each farmer backed his wagon into a stall, paid a fee, and was ready to sell. They had to dawdle with many people who wanted to bargain and get produce as low as possible.

The two top floors of the long building housed the city offices. It was a busy place, and later, I thought how city officials had to fight their way in and out, through stacks and boxes of fruits and vegetables. Across the street were the wholesale commission companies.

The "hucksters" brought their small carts and wagons, often drawn by one skinny horse, and bought produce from us. Then they drove to residential areas and called loudly as they drove up and down the streets, "Canna-loupes! Puhdades! Wadda-melons! Cabbage! Corn!" The women hurried out to the street to look at the sweet corn, pulling back the husks to see if it was well filled, or snapping a green bean to see if it was really fresh.

Oh, it was wonderful, going to market with Papa. When the load was finally sold, we started for home. Sometimes it would be almost noon, and Papa would stop at the grocery store and maybe buy a bag of gingersnaps to hold me until we got home. I always wished he would buy chocolate cookies, but was too timid to say so.

Market Square is gone now, and City Hall is in a fancy building in another area. All the vegetables and fruits are sent in by truck to each grocer. But how wonderful it would be to have a market like we did in the Good Old Days! ❖

CHARLES BERGER

A Weedy Youth

By Gordon Marshall

How Dad hated weeds! Early on I was enlisted in his fight against weeds on our Iowa farm. One of my early memories of work was going along with Dad and my older brother into our horse pasture to kill burdock. It looked like rhubarb, and it thrived in the shade of our large cottonwood trees.

Dad spaded a cut into the pink-and-white root and we boys poured kerosene into the hole.

We three also worked the bluegrass pasture across the creek where Spanish lettuce grew in thick patches. We pulled the white-flowered weeds, stuffed them into burlap sacks and carried them back to the farmyard for burning.

I continued my war on weeds during my grade-school years in the 1930s, battling buffalo burrs, a very thorny, low-growing weed with yellow blossoms, which was devilishly fond of cattle yards and pastures. Brother Stan drove our dirty old Model-A Ford farm car pulling a two-wheeled trailer and I proudly rode on the running board.

Out in the creek pasture we would wheel up to the burr. Wearing leather gloves, I would jump down, pull the weed and throw it into the trailer.

I liked prancing around on that running board, and naturally Stan liked to drive the Model-A. And we took satisfaction in the pile of buffalo burrs that accumulated near the cattle shed and waited to be burned. This job wasn't bad at all!

Gee, maybe I could have been rich! But unknowingly, I destroyed the very low-grade marijuana that grew wild on the farm. In western Iowa, wild hemp thrived along fencerows and especially on creek banks, growing rankly as much as 7 feet tall along our creek. Hemp was a sweaty challenge as we swung a scythe or corn knife on a hot, humid day.

Later, in the 1930s, Dad bought two 80-acre farms some distance from the home place. These tracts had been carelessly farmed, and cockleburs, sunflowers and button weeds had nearly taken over. The first year we farmed the places, the men and we boys marched across the fields like Pickett's charge to pull the noxious weeds.

We also raised bromegrass for seed. The field had to have nearly every weed pulled to qualify as a state-certified seed source. This meant that I pulled a lot of dock and a few other weeds. After the 40-acre field had been in brome for many years, yellow sweet clover became a terrible invader. Sweet clover has a mighty root system and is tough to pull.

One unforgettable year, Dad hired a few town kids to help us, and we pulled sweet clover for a week. Despite leather gloves and young backs, we agreed that that was the worst job yet, even if it did give us a great appetite. The next year we plowed up the field.

Now I'm retired from the farm. When I see our renter roll out his big weed sprayer, I know that I was born too soon. ❖

My Most Unlucky Week

By John G. Mortimer

Some very frustrating incidents are still vivid to me, although they happened when I was about 15. In the summer of 1922, Dad and Mother took a week off from farm work and left my two brothers and me to carry on. My younger brothers were promised a treat if they were good, and I was to judge just how good they were.

My parents' parting words to me were, "Don't let the cows get in the corn." It was the time of year when pasture was no longer palatable and the cattle would walk up and down the fence next to a cornfield, looking for a weak spot to crawl through. It was also time to harvest hay, but if we had to take time to make fences cow-proof, the hay would lose its value for feed. My first job was to save the hay, and I resolved to get so much stored in the barn that Mother and Dad would be pleasantly surprised.

But the first morning we were alone, I had a disappointing delay. The new cement foundation Dad had poured for the cream separator wasn't strong enough. In my haste to crank the machine and speed up the operation, I broke it loose from the foundation and the thing began to stagger like a drunken man.

Our haying came to an abrupt end when the wagon tongue swung violently to one side, striking one of the horses on the flank.

To keep the milk sweet, I carried it to the spring where we kept our butter and cream during hot weather. Then I removed the bolts from the foundation and chiseled out larger holes for them, like a dentist getting ready to fill a tooth. I mixed a richer mixture of concrete to fill the holes, and this time the bolts held.

The field from which we had been hauling hay could be reached only by a steep, rocky trail through the cow pasture. This road, called a dug-way, had some dangerous ditches. It required skill on the driver's part to steer the horses and hay wagon around them and avoid an upset.

Our haying came to an abrupt end when we were coming down the dug-way with a load that almost tipped when the wheels hit a ditch. The wagon tongue swung violently to one side, striking one of the horses on the flank. The jolt broke the wagon tongue.

I unhitched the horses and drove them to the barn. I looked in the pile of lumber we kept for just such emergencies. There were wagon tongues in the rough, but I decided it was beyond my ability to form one of them into a finished tongue.

But I was determined not to give up yet. I could start mowing hay in another field that was much easier to reach. I hitched the horses to the mower and soon had enough cut to make two or three loads. When the hay was ready to haul in, I called our neighbor who lived across the 40 from the field and found that he would let us use his hay wagon. I sent my brothers with the team to get the wagon. I stayed in the field, piling the hay by hand because we had no hay loader. I often glanced in the direction the boys had gone, but there was no sign of them or the horses. I was getting uneasy; clouds were gathering in the west, and I worried that our hay might get wet.

Just as my patience was wearing thin, I saw the team and wagon coming around the barn. When they drove into the field, I asked the boys, "What took you kids so long? Can't you see we have to get his hay in before it rains?"

They confessed that they had been reading the funnies. This was the worst thing that my brothers did that week, and I resolved to report this to the folks and tell them that I didn't think they deserved a surprise.

The next interruption came as we were taking a forkful of hay from the load into the barn. Just as it reached the peak and was moving toward the back of the barn, two sections of the track came apart and the carriage came off the track. The carriage and the forkful of hay fell just inside the big door.

I was able to retrieve everything except one small wheel. My next move was to visit the neighboring farms to try to locate the missing part. After calling on a number of neighbors, I turned for home. There was one place I had missed on the way out—and of course, they had just what I needed.

I didn't look forward to building a makeshift ladder from the beam to the peak of the barn to make the repair. I had to be very sure that it would hold my weight. I was more afraid of heights then than I am now. But I finally got the ladder built, and I climbed up to loosen the clamps that held the track. When I had worked the track back into place and repositioned the carrier on the track, we were ready again for business.

And what about those cows? Well, they did find a hole in the fence, and made one cornfield look like hail had struck it. I felt regretful when I had to tell Dad and Mother about the corn, and when I reported the boys for reading the funnies when they should have been helping with the hay. I was not very happy when I saw how disappointed they were. ❖

Life on a Rotating Handle

By Allen Benton

As I look back on my farm childhood, it seems I spent an inordinate amount of time on the rotating handles of farm implements.

Running a water pump, a grindstone, a fanning mill, a corn sheller—all jobs that today are performed by electricity—were done by hand, and usually the hand of a boy. It required no particular skill and not much strength to turn the handles.

There was one exception, however. The flail, a device for threshing grain, required a great deal of skill. One had to grasp its handle and perform a rotary motion, so skill was necessary.

In case you have never seen or used one, a flail consisted of two round pieces of hardwood about 1½ inches in diameter. The handle was perhaps 4 or 5 feet long, and the beater, which was connected to the handle by a rotating device, was 2–2½ feet.

One of us would feed the ears of corn into the maw of this cast-iron monster while the other turned the handle.

I grasped the handle with both hands and rotated the forward hand so as to make the beater swing in an arc. If I made an injudicious movement, I cracked my knuckles. It was even possible to whack myself in the head—but this required a major miscalculation.

The trick was to rotate the handle in such a way that the beater could be brought to the floor flat with considerable force against the grain. After a few minutes of this treatment, most of the kernels had been released from the husks so I could clear away the straw with a pitchfork and shovel up the grain.

Threshed grain, whether flailed or run through a threshing machine, always contains a certain amount of chaff. Biblical injunctions about separating the grain from the chaff were very real to us. The job was done with an infernal device known as a fanning mill.

This large, complex wooden contraption had a large trough on top, into which a couple of bushels of grain could be dumped. Turning the handle accomplished two things. The trough moved from side to side, and the grain moved down its sloped boards and cascaded off into a series of screens.

The handle was also attached to an axle that rotated a large wooden fan, housed in the bulging end of the mill. As the grain was screened, the fan blew husks and unfilled kernels out the back. Usually the device was placed so the chaff was blown right out the barn door to be carried away on the breeze. Meanwhile, the screened and winnowed grain fell through a screen into a drawer at the bottom.

The fanning mill occupied a lot of my time because we grew our own grain for the livestock. Every week or two we had to put up grist—bags of different kinds of grain to take to the gristmill.

After winnowing the wheat, oats and barley, I would likely move a few feet along the barn floor and tackle the corn sheller. Since this was harder work and required two people, my older brother and I took turns. One of us would feed the ears of corn into the maw of this cast-iron monster while the other turned the handle.

Inside, rasping plates grated the corn off the cob and cast the shelled cobs out a hole at the side. The shelled corn poured out of an opening at the bottom, landing in a bucket. It then had to be transferred to a bag and added to the grist we were to take to the mill.

My days of rotating handles started early in the morning with the cream separator. Selling whole milk required more sanitation and inspection than we were prepared to handle, so we sold only the cream to a butter-and-cheese factory nearby. After each milking, we had to spend a half-hour or so whirling the handle of the cream separator at high speed so that the cream came out of one spout and the skim milk out of the other. Then followed the tiresome job of washing and sterilizing the separator parts to be ready for the next milking.

One of the least-pleasant jobs was turning the handle of the grindstone while my father or brother sharpened the mowing-machine knives, the scythe or, as the season for butchering approached, the butcher knives. This job was especially nasty because it took place in the heat of summer. Even though we placed the grindstone in the shade of a large chestnut tree, a boy could very quickly work up a sweat. It took a long time to sharpen the two sides of a 6-foot row of mowing-machine blades; I was always thoroughly tired long before the job was done.

We had two kinds of pumps in those days, both hand-operated. Only one—the chain pump—rotated. It had a chain which formed a complete circle and was placed over a cogged wheel at the top, on the axle of the handle. At intervals the chain had rubber devices which passed through a square wooden tube on their way up, carrying water upward. This worked even if the well was so deep that a pump operating strictly on vacuum would not work.

In the warmer months, we had to pump water only for domestic use. In winter, however, when the snow was so deep that the livestock could not reach the pond or spring, we had to pump enough water to satisfy their needs, too. A cow could live for a while without water, but she wouldn't produce milk, so daily watering was essential.

It didn't matter what the weather conditions were; we had to stand at the well and turn the handle for a couple of hours, often in a howling wind with the snow swirling around us. The cows were let out two or three at a time and allowed their turn at the large iron kettle, before they were driven back to the barn to make room for the next batch.

One more device with a rotating handle played a large part in my childhood: the butter churn. Actually, we had several kinds of churns, some with rotating handles and some with dashers that were driven up and down.

Some days the cream showed a marked reluctance to be transformed into butter, and the churning went on for what seemed like an interminable period. I always liked butter, but I certainly did not enjoy making it.

I suppose that most farm children of the years since the 1930s are mercifully unfamiliar with these instruments of torture. But to the farm boy of prewar days, they were a constant part of a difficult and spartan life. ❖

Down on the Farm

By Harrison Flash

Down on the farm, 'bout half past four
I slip on my pants and sneak out the door
Out to the barn I run like the dickens
To milk ten cows and feed the chickens
Clean out the barn, curry Nancy and Jiggs
Separate the cream and feed the pigs
Work two hours, then eat like a Turk
And by heck, I'm ready for a full day's work.

Then I grease the wagon and put on the rack
Throw a jug of water in an old grain sack
Hitch up the horses, hustle down the lane
Must get the hay in, for it looks like rain
Look over yonder, sure as I'm born
Cattle's on the rampage and cows in the corn
Start across the medder, run a mile or two
Heaving like I'm windbroke, get wet clean through
Get back to the horses, then for recompense
Nance gets straddle the barbwire fence
Joints all a aching and muscles in a jerk
I'm fit as a fiddle for a full day's work.

Work all summer till winter is nigh
Then figure up the books and heave a big sigh
Worked all year, didn't make a thing
Got less cash than I did last spring
Now some people say that there ain't no hell
But they never farmed, so how can they tell
When spring rolls around I take another chance
While the fringe grows longer on my old work pants
Give my s'penders a hitch, my belt another jerk
And by heck, I'm ready for a full day's work.

Saturday's Child

By Ruby L. Anders

Each child in our family had a specific chore to do on Saturday before he was free to enjoy his own pursuits.

The older boys did chores around the barn while 10-year-old Carl filled the huge wood box on the side porch.

Myra's job was to clean the corner cupboard in the dining room where Mama kept the good china. Myra actually enjoyed handling the fragile china that was painted with red roses and green leaves. We all knew the story of how the china came clear across three states in a barrel of flour in a wagon driven by our grandfather. Our grandmother, it seems, had hidden the china in the flour without Grandpa's knowledge.

Myra also loved to clean the tall, thin goblets that Papa had bought Mama as a surprise one time when he took the cattle into the city to market. Carefully, she wiped out the tall goblets with the gold bands and carefully she put fresh paper in the shelves before returning the dishes to their places.

Kate dusted every piece of furniture with O'Cedar furniture polish until you could see yourself in it, and Mary Nelle polished mirrors and lamp chimneys until they gleamed.

I gladly would have traded jobs with any of them because my Saturday job was to clean the huge black cookstove that graced the corner of our kitchen. Mother was strict about that stove, vowing it would have to last a lifetime, and it very nearly did.

The Home Comfort, as the stove was called, was our only source of cooking and also our source of heat for the kitchen and dining room. The only trouble was it gave out heat both in summer and winter. The stove was appreciated most of all in the winter on Saturday nights when the tub was brought in for our weekly baths. But to me, who had to clean it, it looked like a black monster, and every Saturday I eyed it with loathing. Particularly I hated the job because, while the others could be finished with their tasks by noon, I had to wait until Mama had finished Saturday's baking and the midday meal was over, and the stove could cool off.

First I shook down the wood ashes. We had lots of timber, so we didn't burn coal, and we emptied the ashes outside in the chicken lot so the chickens could scratch in them. Then I dipped out any water left in the reservoir attached to the side of the stove and wiped the reservoir clean.

Next, I lifted the shining nickel-plated trim from the front of the stove and shined it with Bon-Ami. The warming oven with the pipe running through it had to be washed with sudsy water and carefully dried to prevent rusting.

Then I was ready for the Black Silk stove polish, and I always finished with a good supply of it under my fingernails. It didn't come out until I had washed my hands several times. I always tried to keep my hands hidden at Sunday school the next day.

While the polish dried, I filled the reservoir with fresh water and laid a fire for the evening meal. Then with a soft cloth, I polished the stove to a fare-thee-well.

With relief, I replaced the nickel-plated trim, washed my hands and stood impatiently by while Mama inspected the stove. When she smiled her approval and gave me a couple of fresh baked cookies, I was free to go join my friend, Ruth, to enjoy what was left of the Saturday afternoon. Somehow, I never caught the glow of accomplishment that Myra and the others did for a job well done.

But it wasn't until after Myra got married and I inherited her job and Kate took over the stove that I realized it wasn't such a bad job, and more in my line. Somehow, handling that china gave me the willies. I was glad to pass it on to the next in line. ❖

Getting in the Hay

By Hulda E. Hill

*I*t looked like another long, hot day coming. For a month, the relentless sun had baked an already brown world, with only a couple of quick thundershowers that brought just enough dampness to settle the dust.

Quietly sliding off the straw mattress so as not to disturb my two sisters who were still sleeping, I looked out the window. At 5:30 the sun was rising in a blaze of red, orange and pink in the eastern sky. Hitching up my bloomers, I reached for my overalls that hung on one of the bedposts and quickly pulled them on. As I pushed the brass buttons through the metal buckles on the shoulder straps, my eye caught the merest glimpse of a gray cloud on the western horizon.

Hmm, that cloud looks kinda like rain, I thought to myself. Maybe I can get a better look from the other window.

My bare feet made no noise as I walked between the two beds to stand up on tiptoe in order to see out through the top pane. The lower one was covered with cheesecloth to keep the flies and mosquitoes out.

A few dark, billowy clouds rose in the west. Forgetting the sleeping girls in the two beds, I let out a sigh of relief. We needed a good rain to cool the hot, dry air and bring some green to the scorched fields.

Pa came in from the barn and went to the bottom of the stairs. "Hey, the sun is shining! But not for long. To the hayfield, everybody!"

"Get out of here, so people can sleep," Ida mumbled out of her pillow.

"I'm going, I'm going," I answered. "Betcha Pa calls all of you up to get on the hayfield! There's some clouds coming up."

A tennis shoe came flying after me as I went through the boys' room to the stairs.

"In the meantime, you can hush up 'til he does call us," Ed groaned, burying his head under his pillow and going back to sleep.

"Well, look who's up so early." Ma poked at the fire with the lid lifter, prodding at a stick of stovewood to make it go down deep into the hot embers.

"Where's Pa?"

"He went to get the cows into the barn. Why don't you run to the woodshed and get an armload of stove wood? I used up all there was to make that rieska (a flat Finnish bread made with rye or other dark flour) and now I want to fry some pancakes for breakfast."

A gentle wind fanned the leaves on the apple tree. The grass rippled in waves along the path as I ran to the woodshed. The colors in the sky were fading fast as the sun appeared fully, casting long shadows on the ground. A robin hopped in the weeds near the sauna, stopping every few feet to listen for worms. It sang a vigorous, chirpy melody. Maybe it, too, felt the oncoming rain.

Filling my arms with pieces of wood off the neat stacks piled in the shed, I returned to the kitchen and dumped them into the wood box. Now I could have my morning cup of cocoa. From the cupboard near the dish table, I took out the box of Ambrosia cocoa, reached up to the middle shelf for the big enamel cup, and taking a spoon from the cupboard drawer, took them to the table.

With the boys working on one side of the wagon and Pa on the other, the load was stacking up fast.

"Let me pour that hot water for you," Ma said. "It's boiling hot."

To the hot water I added the cocoa, sugar and the last of the milk from the cream pitcher. There were some sheets of rieska cooling off in a towel on the table. I broke off a piece and buttered it to eat with the cocoa.

"Don't be eating that now," said Ma. "You heard me say there's going to be pancakes."

"But I only took a small piece. I like it when it's warm."

Pa came in from the barn and went to the bottom of the stairs. "Hey, the sun is shining! But not for long. To the hayfield, everybody!"

Small groans of protest sounded as feet hit the floor upstairs. Yawning and rubbing their eyes, Ed and Bert came down and went on through the kitchen and out the door. As Ed walked past me, I stuck out my tongue at him and whispered, "See, I told you he'd get you up!" He made a move to smack me, but changed his mind, remembering that Father was near.

We could hear the girls getting up, so Ma moved the heavy, black frying pan over the fire. Checking the damper on the stovepipe and reaching down the side of the stove to close the draught, she was ready to cook the pancakes.

Helen set the table while the little boys filled the wood box. The big boys were told to get some water to fill the stove boiler and the tea kettle.

The stack of pancakes grew high on the platter in the warming oven. On the table, a crock of butter joined the sugar bowls in the center, along with an economy-size bottle of Karo syrup. Old plates and an assortment of cups and glasses and mismatched knives and forks were set at each place.

The milk was cooling in the well in an 8-pound lard pail which was suspended from a nail on a piece of clothesline to water level. The well was 25 feet deep with rock-lined walls and a wooden platform over the top. In the center of the platform, a raised, boxlike structure had a lid which was held down between uses by a heavy rock.

Helen lifted the rock off the lid and set it aside. She felt the welcome coolness rise up as she pulled hand over hand on the rope. Untying the clothesline from the pail handle, she reached to close the well cover when the screen door banged shut behind her.

"Let it be!" Bert yelled, running down the steps with the water pails. "We'll close it after we haul the water." Ed was right behind him with another pail swinging in his hand.

Picking up her milk pail, Helen watched her brothers hook the long sapling pole to the handle of a pail and lower it to dip a bucket of water and haul it up again.

"Boy, I sure wish we'd get a rain. Look how low that water is down there." Ed wiped his hands on the back of his overalls. "Heard Uncle Matt has to haul all their water from the spring in his lower field. Makes this haymaking harder, too; it's so hot and dusty in the fields."

Helen held the screen door open for her brothers as they slopped in with the water. Swishing away the flies, she made sure the door was closed all the way.

The pancakes were being served as Pa and the little boys started to eat. Jack and Evert were the younger boys, close enough in age and looks that they were often mistaken for twins. Barefoot, hair cut to the scalp, and dressed in the same type of overalls as Pa and the big boys wore, the two sat next to each other on the bench, brown as berries. Slingshots hung from their back pockets.

I got in next to Jack, buttered the little boys' pancakes, poured syrup over them, cut them in bite-sized pieces, and then attacked my own meal.

Pa had started eating as we kids did the chores, and was now on his second cup of coffee. He poured the liquid from the cup into a deep saucer. Helping himself to a lump of sugar, he placed it on his tongue, then sipped at the hot coffee from the saucer.

He spoke only Finnish, although he understood English. At age 46, his years of hard labor showed in his work-roughened hands. Yet he stood straight. His blue eyes, his black hair that showed no sign of gray, and his ready smile belied his years. Raising a family of nine children in those Depression years, he worked at any job he could find.

He set his saucer down as the big boys slid down to eat. A pack of Peerless came out of his back pocket. He opened the folded ends of foil wrap and dug out a generous chew of tobacco.

"Feels like rain coming, so eat quickly now, and we will try to get in all the hay that we raked yesterday. You little girls come, too, after you wash those dishes." He went out to hitch the borrowed team to the wagon that stood by the hay barn.

Leaving Ma to run the milk through the cream separator, Helen and I got at the dishes. When all the breakfast and separator dishes were washed, dried and put away, I went to empty the dishwater into the ferns behind the house.

I could see Pa and the big boys stacking hay onto the high wagon, working on the run. Great clouds closed in overhead, and I could see it was already raining on the Tapiola side of the lake.

Running into the house, I slammed the dishpan inside the other one under the dish table on a shelf and told Helen to hurry. "I'll run and get the rakes from the barn. Let's go!"

With the boys working on one side of the wagon and Pa on the other, the load was stacking up fast. As Helen and I ran up with our rakes, Pa hollered, "One of you get up on the load and trample it down. We need only one to rake."

Helen took my rake from me and leaned it against a haystack. "You get up there, and I'll rake. I can go faster than you."

For a second I forgot our need to hurry and opened my mouth to tell her to quit acting smart again. Pa walked toward the wagon with a big bunch of hay on his pitchfork. Tossing it up on top of the load he said, "No time to quibble—GET!"

Scrambling up on one end of the wagon, I muttered to myself, "I'll get that smarty. You watch, I'll get her when Ma or Pa ain't around, and she won't act so high hat."

Taking up the pitchfork that was standing in the middle of the load, I spread the hay evenly, trampling it down with my small weight. Dodging each new bunch that Pa and the boys tossed up there kept me on my toes. With one eye on my work and one on the threatening sky, I saw that there was room on the wagon for the three remaining stacks. When Pa went for the last pile, he had Helen hold the rake that had been leaning against it.

"Now, Ed and I will get this to the barn while the rest of you finish raking what is left. Bert can carry it to the barn. Hurry, we need you there to move this hay and trample it down."

Working like beavers, we three raked the area clean where the stacks had stood. We had been doing this for a week now, so without any talk, the loose hay was gathered into one pile. Bert impaled it on his pitchfork, raised it over his shoulder and started toward the barn. Helen and I, with only the rakes to carry, ran on ahead. The slow team was just pulling up to the barn doors as we put away our rakes and climbed into the haymow. Bert came around the end of the wagon and threw his bundle of hay as far back as his short, 13-year-old height could reach, then joined Helen and me on top of the hay.

As Pa and Ed unloaded the wagon into the building, it was Bert's job to move it farther back and ours to spread it evenly and trample it down.

As we worked, lightning started to flash. The thunderclaps were frightening. We heard the chickens run cackling toward their roost in a corner of the cow barn. The men worked faster as the first few drops of rain splashed down. By the time the last of the load was in, the water was coming in windblown sheets. Leaving Pa and Ed to unhitch the horses, we kids ran for the shelter of the house. ❖

Berrying Time

By Barbara Rice

There's an old pasture near my home in Crown Point, N.Y. It's overgrown with juniper bushes and small cedar trees. My grandmother, Leda, and I called this place Breed's Pasture, after the farmer who owned it.

One hot summer in my early childhood, Grandma Leda and I spent many hours picking berries in this pasture—strawberries in June, then blackberries in August. To reach them, we had to cross a small bridge that spanned a sluggish creek. We'd climb an old-fashioned stile at the far end of the garden.

In June, the strawberries grew in profusion on the fertile ground near a large wood lot. With our shining new berry pails, we always competed to see who could gather the most berries, watching out for the cattle that often grazed near the fence.

On the trip home, we didn't always choose the route leading across the creek. Sometimes we took the picturesque wood road that ran through a hemlock grove. We heard the complaining cries of baby crows and the breathtaking songs of the veery and wood thrush.

Later on, in August, my grandmother and I set out again with empty pails—this time to pick blackberries in the same pasture. The blackberry patch was inside a large, grassy meadow, separated from the main pasture by a wooden fence to keep the cows out.

In order to reach it, we followed a steep, winding path that ran downhill to a spot where the fence boards were broken through and rotted away. To my child's eyes, the wide, grassy meadow beyond was beautiful. Daisies, devil's paintbrush and black-eyed Susans dotted the field. Grandma Leda and I crossed this meadow to reach the denser part of the blackberry briars.

We picked the big, juicy berries that hung to the ground with the same zest for competition that we'd had in June, a slight mist hung over Breed's Pasture, hinting of autumn's approach.

At the end of these berry trips, we were rewarded for our efforts, when we sat down at the supper table and enjoyed the homemade goodness of fresh berry pie. ❖

The Hard Way

By Francis G. "Bud" Morrison

In 1922, when I was 9 years old, our family of seven moved from Norfolk to an 11-acre farm near Virginia Beach. My father had just retired from the Navy, and like so many retired servicemen, wanted to be a "gentleman farmer."

We had about half an acre of yard, about 4½ acres each of fruit trees and strawberries, and the rest, which we called "the wilderness," was occupied by a tangle of gooseberries, blackberries, weeds and a scuppernong grape arbor. The heavy "trunk" of the grapevine curved to make a natural seat about 2 feet off the ground with dense foliage overhead.

This was my secret summer retreat. When we couldn't get a ballgame going, I could sit there and read about the Land of Oz, the Motor Boys, the Boy Allies, the Rover Boys, Tarzan and his animal buddies and more, letting my imagination run wild.

A few months after we moved to the farm, the strawberry crop began to ripen. Dad hired pickers at two cents per quart. They carried trays holding 10 one-quart containers into the fields and brought them back to Dad full of luscious, ripe strawberries. A good picker could turn in as many as 10 trays in a day, earning a cool $2. I had never earned money before, and this seemed a good place to start. So, after I pleaded some, Dad agreed to let me pick and pay me the going rate. Wow!

I guess I've always been competitive, being one of five siblings, and even though I was a kid with no experience, I wanted to pick as many berries as the old hands did. In the process, I learned a lesson that has stayed with me for a lifetime.

The only way I could keep up with the veteran pickers was to pick almost every strawberry in my row—ripe, unripe, overripe or damaged. When I had filled my first tray and brought it back to Dad, expecting compliments for my fast work, I got a rude shock. I knew I hadn't quite followed orders to pick only the healthy, ripe berries, but what the heck! I was the boss's son, wasn't I? Dad would surely overlook a little fudging. Boy, was I wrong!

After inspecting one quart, he put the whole tray aside and told me I should be ashamed of myself. The fact that I was new at berry picking didn't "cut any ice," as he put it. He told me that as his son, instead of trying to get by with shoddy work, I should try to set an example for the other pickers.

He told me to empty my containers one at a time and throw out all of the overripe and damaged fruit, refilling as many containers as possible with the good berries and the other baskets with the unripe ones. Then he would pay me 2 cents a quart for the good ones and charge me a penny for the "greenies." So, instead of two dimes, I earned only eight cents while losing valuable picking time.

You might consider that a hard lesson for a 9-year-old, but I learned something important: It's not how much you do in this world that counts; it's how well you do it. ❖

Herding

By Ina Chambers

Back in the days when the larger part of our population were farm folks, children's pastimes were dictated by necessity. On many farms, children spent their summers "herding."

What did they herd? On the prairie farm where I spent most of my childhood, the youngsters herded milk cows, range steers or sheep. Fences were few, and it would not do to let livestock wander too far afield. The small acreage under fence was reserved for Sundays and holidays, when the children were relieved of their tedious chore.

Later, when I was living in the Ozarks, I drove a fair-sized flock of ducks down to the bank of Curley Creek every morning, and allowed them to enter the water to dive and dart and swim. Each mama duck took her little ones downstream to the line that divided our farm from Farmer Brown's land. At that point, I forced them to swim back upstream to the confinement of their pen.

Under these circumstances, there was no lack of "children's activities." Our modest ranch supported not only a thousand head of our own sheep, but another thousand that belonged to a "Main Street farmer" (yes, we had them in those days, too).

After an early breakfast, the first thing we did was open the corral gate and let our own herd in to the water trough. Their thirst slaked, they were herded onto the open range, one youngster behind them. Then the gate to the other corral was opened and the sheep we were boarding were let out. They, too, were herded onto the range after drinking, but in a slightly different direction, so that the herds could be kept

Our parents were not aware of how far the little fellow traveled until a neighboring rancher spoke to my father about it one day.

separate. Another youngster guided this flock. Then we were on our own for the day.

The required equipment for a day of herding consisted of a heavy stick for killing rattlesnakes, a canteen of water and a lunch in a paper bag. In addition, we carried the makings for a simple tent for shelter from the hot prairie sun, and some sort of a digging tool—usually a broken kitchen knife.

Of course, our first task was keeping the sheep on good grass without letting them go too far astray. But the greater responsibility was making sure the herds did not mix. If a lamb from one flock strayed into the other, that evening Father would have to listen for the mixed-up lamb crying for its mother. The answering "Baa" from the other flock told him which ewe was missing her baby, and the lamb was restored to its mother.

Herding cattle was different. At one time, Father had a herd of steers he planned on grazing until fall, when they would go into the feed yards. He worked away from home, and while open range was all around the homestead, there were no fences to keep the animals from wandering away as they grazed. Father bought a little Indian pony for his 8-year-old son, and Johnnie was commissioned to know at all times where the steers were pasturing. Sometimes Johnnie's love of adventure took him in the wrong direction. He might wander far afield, and many times night overtook him before he located the steers and returned home. But his beloved little Hiawatha always brought him safely back to the homestead.

Our parents were not aware of how far the

little fellow traveled until a neighboring rancher spoke to my father about it one day. "One day last week I saw Johnnie over on Dobe Creek (23 miles from home), looking for those steers. Don't you worry about him?"

"No," Father replied. "He enjoys his riding, he has a trusty little pony, and we have taught him to beware of rattlesnakes. He knows enough to leave them alone and never try to kill them."

That was what he thought—but one evening Johnnie rode in without shoes and only one bridle rein. A rattlesnake had struck at his pony, and that was more than Johnnie could accept without a scrap. Without dismounting, he had taken off a rein and attempted to kill the snake by beating it with the metal snap. The snap caught in the body of the snake and Johnnie had no choice but to drop the rein.

Then he took off his shoes, one after the other, and threw them at the snake. Since Father had told him never to dismount to kill a rattler, he seemed to have no choice but to come home without his shoes or the bridle rein.

Herding the milk cows was another matter, and that was a chore left to the girls of the family. My first piece of needlework, a little linen centerpiece, was embroidered while herding the milk cows during a summer forenoon. I still use it. We gathered wildflowers. We pulled wild onions to eat with our lunch, in spite of loud protests from other members of the family who swore our breath was worse than the smell of skunks.

When we moved to the Ozark Mountains in 1910, we learned the method the hill folk used to get their turkeys to market. They herded them there. Starting at the little farm farthest from market, the owner left the farm, driving his turkeys before him, very early in the morning. Each turkey was distinctively marked, either with a leg band or a turkey bell. As the driver advanced, his flock was joined by other owners and flocks. The herd increased in size until the market was reached.

Years later, back on the prairie, my husband and I tried our hand at herding turkeys. It was during the mid-1930s, when farmers were plagued not only by the Depression, but by a drought that did not allow a crop to be grown for eight years. It seemed the only "assets" we had were cacti and grasshoppers. We turned to raising turkeys for a cash crop. Though we had raised no feed or grain, nature provided us with free turkey feed.

Every afternoon at about 4 o'clock, we herded our flock of young poults out onto the open prairie where thousands of voracious grasshoppers jumped about in the short, stunted grass, burned brown by the sun. The turkeys gobbled them hungrily, and by the time the fowl had been herded a quarter of a mile, their crops were so full of hoppers that they almost dragged on the ground. Then they were herded back to the pens.

While our sheep were barely subsisting on cacti with the spines burned off, the turkeys were growing fat on grasshoppers. Thus did nature provide when the rains failed to come.

Whether we herded sheep, cattle or poultry, those days on the farm were tough, but carefree and rewarding! ❖

Alone on the Range

By Edna Krause

Back when I was 8 years old and what they called a "puny kid," I was given an unusual job that lasted six summers. I liked my job because it was more fun than thinning sugar beets with my older brothers and sisters.

My brothers, Eddie and Stanley, teased me and called me "the cowherdess." It sounded horrible and it upset me until my sister, Cel, who was a teacher, explained, "If shepherds tend sheep and you tend cows, then you are a cowherdess."

Well then, a cowherdess I was. And that was because adjacent to our farm in Upper Michigan were miles and miles of state land, all unfenced. I watched the cattle every day from the third week in May until Labor Day, I kept the cows from wandering away.

How I remember those long, leisurely days! As the herd grazed contentedly or chewed their cuds in the cool shade, I amused myself in a variety of ways.

If Becky, my dog, was still with me, I'd play a form of hide-and-seek with her. But more often than not, she'd sneak back home without my seeing her leave.

The cows were like people to me. I especially remember Reddy, who looked up at me from her munching whenever I talked to her. And there was Blacky, whom I hugged and petted because she had no horns and was so gentle. And how could I forget the two oldest cows—Grandma and Grandpa!

Each new summer month brought forth a variety of delicious wild fruit. The wintergreens were first to dot the lowlands with their bright red berries. If berries were scarce, I nibbled on the minty wintergreen leaves.

Strawberries were my favorite food. Wild cherries were small and sour. Then there were the prickly wild gooseberries that were so luscious—if you could stand the pain of biting open the skin and squeezing out the sweet, juicy centers.

I amused myself by making daisy chains from dandelion stems. I gathered up an apronful of the bright yellow blossoms, selecting the ones with the longest stems. Then I snapped off the yellow heads and began my loops.

If I wanted more vigorous exercise, I climbed almost to the top of a small poplar tree. By rocking the tree I created a whipping effect that propelled me back and forth through the air.

Sometimes my brother Eddie loaned me his jackknife and I made a poplar whistle. Selecting a 1½-inch-diameter branch with smooth bark, I cut off a 6-inch length. By removing the bark and carving a couple of niches, I made a whistle.

Occasionally the herd grazed along either side of the narrow, gravel road that ran between our farm and the state farm. Then I walked ahead of the animals, drawing figures on the smooth surfaces of the road with a stick. Or, if the horse-drawn road grader had gone through recently, I hunted for pretty stones in the gravel.

When the cattle grazed along the sides of the road I had my greatest responsibility. Sometimes an old Model-T would putt-putt down the road. Then it was my job to keep the animals from ambling across the road in front of the car.

The only time cowherding was more crucial was when the botfly (sometimes called the heel fly) buzzed over the herd. Then nothing stopped them from stampeding! It was useless and dangerous to try to divert them from their path of escape from the stinging parasite. However, a car seldom went down this bumpy road, and stampedes were rare.

So that is how I spent six happy summers. I was alone on the range, but too busy to be lonely. ❖

Here, Bossy!

By Patricia Sherman

Here, Bossy! Come here, Bossy!" It was milking time and the two milk cows were out in the pasture.

I climbed halfway up the ladder on the windmill. From there I couldn't see forever, but I could see most of the pasture and locate the herd. We had nine cattle, including the two milk cows.

"Here, Bossy! Here, Bossy!" They didn't listen to me, a 12-year-old girl. The old, bossy cows kept on grazing. I had to go after them, but at least I knew what direction to go. Climbing that windmill saved me many a step.

Before the day I thought about climbing it, I used to traipse all over the place, looking for the cattle. Sometimes they were resting in the grove of trees, and sometimes they grazed behind the plum thicket.

After jumping down from the last step, I picked up my stick and hustled off to round up the herd. Just like the postman, come rain or shine, 110 degrees or a blizzard, I had to go get those cows. My father insisted that it was my evening chore.

I hurried on cold winter days. In the summer I sauntered, pretending that the pasture flowers were part of an Austrian meadow until I made my way behind the cattle. Then, when I hollered a few "hey yas!" and waved my stick, they would fall into a parade line toward the barn. I needed only the two milk cows, but where one went, the rest followed.

I dropped into the back of the line, and as they chewed their cuds, I chewed bubble gum. Sometimes a young calf would fall behind, and I would stroke its forehead and pat its shoulders before making it run to catch the others.

Back at the barn, my ranching duties ended until it was time to use the cream separator. Mother milked the cows. I wanted to, but she didn't want a dried-up cow. My hands were not strong enough to milk. So while she milked, I played with the cats that were sitting close by, waiting for their portion of the milk.

Originally, it had been my sister's job to find the cows and bring them in. But when she got married and left the farm, the chore fell to me. At first, it was exciting; I was part of the ranching process. Then it got boring, and I decided it was very unladylike.

While walking behind the cows, I often daydreamed about living in the city—no chores! No eggs to gather, no cream separator to turn, no hay to put into the feeders, and no yelling, "Hey yas!" What a life I thought that would be! But I was stuck. I was too young to marry.

Then I began to daydream about the farm girl changing into a city princess. And poof! It seemed to come true. The farm was sold and my parents bought a house in town. I got an education. I got a white princess dress and was married.

With my prince of a husband, I moved on to the big city. I was free at last. No more watching where I stepped in the pasture. No more looking for snakes before I reached into a hen's nest. No more summer breezes gently blowing the windmill. No wildflowers to pick for the table. No wobbly baby calves to touch and love. No more trusting cows with brown eyes and velvet noses. Ahhhh … "Here, Bossy!" ❖

Winter Chores

By Jack M. Harmon

Winter mornings started out by thawing the pump. We had seven head of stock—five milk cows, a bull and a steer—plus 60 chickens. All of these animals and birds required huge quantities of water that had to be carried both night and morning. I would get a bucket of hot water from the kitchen, thaw the pump and draw the first of 15 or 20 buckets to the barn. The problem was that by the time I got back to the well, that darn pump was frozen solid again.

Then I climbed to the loft and threw down the day's supply of hay and bedding. After that, it was off to the granary for feed.

After feeding the cattle their ration of grain, I got another bucket of warm water from the kitchen and washed down the milkers' bags and teats. I didn't mind milking in the winter. I didn't get smacked by the cows' tails as they fought flies, and it was kind of comforting to press my head against Bossy's warm side.

After the milk had been strained and put down to cool, I cleaned the stables and spread fresh bedding. Then, off to the house we went for breakfast.

At night we banked the fires with a little coal and filled the reservoirs on both cookstoves.

Ma always had a big tub of hot water, a bar of fragrant soap and our house shoes waiting for us in the summer kitchen. She saw to it that we got washed up and out of our barn clothes before coming to the table. "Just because you're a farmer, you don't have to smell like a barn," she told us more than once.

Breakfast consisted of big platters of hotcakes, eggs, ham, bacon or sausage, a big jug of syrup, a tub of fresh churned butter and cold milk, all crowned by sweet rolls and gallons of fresh, hand-ground coffee.

Both Ma and Pa believed in eating a big breakfast. Pa used to say, "If you eat a hearty breakfast you won't suffer too much if you miss lunch or if supper is a little late."

After breakfast and before I went out to check my trap line, I had to fill the three wood boxes—one in the kitchen, one in the setting room and one in the summer kitchen.

At night we banked the fires with a little coal and filled the reservoirs on both cookstoves. This way we had plenty of hot water for the next morning. In addition, I had to carry two buckets of water each for the kitchen and summer kitchen. This, too, was for the morning's use and was also available in case of fire.

Wednesday afternoon was my day to go to the feed mill. I had to fire up the tractor, load the wagon with corn and oats and drive 6 miles to the feed mill. In the winter it seemed like an endless journey. Even with two pairs of pants, a sheepskin coat, gloves, hat and muffler, it was a cold trip.

I had two options: I could poke along and prolong the agony, or I could stick the tractor in fifth gear, get battered by the wind and chance sliding off the snow-covered road. The tractors didn't have cabs in those days, so by the time the grain was ground and I got back home, I had lost all feeling in my hands and feet.

Back to those wood stoves. We cut most of

our firewood in early winter. It took a lot of wood to fire three stoves, plus we needed wood for the smokehouse and the sugar shanty. After awhile I got into the rhythm of the big crosscut saw; it wasn't too bad if the person on the other end was experienced and did not try to fight its swing. Splitting was quite another matter. Anyone who tells you that splitting half-frozen oak isn't hard work … well, they just have never done it.

A few months prior to plowing, usually in late January, we started building and repairing fences. We started a hole with a bar, but even with this pilot hole, driving a fencepost into half-frozen ground was a chore. We loaded the wagon with posts, a roll of barbed wire, a bucket of staples, a fence maul, claw hammers and fence pliers.

That fencing wagon was like any other wagon except it had two of Pa's inventions. On one side he had put a hinged platform to stand on while driving the posts. On the back he had rigged up a reel-type arrangement. A roll of barbed wire was dropped into it and a chunk of pipe acted like a brake. As the tractor and wagon pulled forward, the wire stretched out behind and the brake controlled the tension. This was a lot better than stretching wire with a block and tackle.

Even with Pa's invention, I never got through a day of fencing without numerous cuts on my hands, arms and legs. Ma had a big job patching and repairing the rips and tears in our jackets and jeans. We could always tell when a neighbor was fencing by the condition of his clothes and the bandages and smell of horse liniment on his hands and arms. Fencing was not one of my favorite winter jobs.

At least twice during the winter a blizzard would hit. Between the endless snow and the wind, if things didn't come to a stop, they at least down-shifted into a lower gear.

Pa had rigged a blade on the front of the tractor and it worked fine for clearing the drives and the barn lot. There was still plenty of shoveling to do, though—the paths to the chicken house, the smokehouse, the milk house and the privy. The fun part was that after I had

cleared 40 or 50 feet, I would look back to see that the wind had blown the path full again.

Some winters, it was more than a week before anyone could get to town or the mailman or milk truck could get through This wasn't much of a hardship, except the cattle were put on half a grain ration. But they could fill up on extra hay. When the milk truck didn't get through, Ma made butter and cottage cheese from the excess.

Ma kept the cupboards well stocked so we always had plenty to eat. The smokehouse was loaded with hams, bacon and links of sausages. She made a big crock of kraut each fall and gallons of pickles.

The bins in the root cellar overflowed with potatoes, carrots, turnips and parsnips, and the shelves bulged with jars of cold-packed beef and deer meat. She canned and dried corn and had hundreds of quarts of fruits and vegetables. No, we didn't go hungry. Ma loved to cook and she could toss together a meal in no time at all, one that was fit for a king—or even everyday company.

I still remember those winter suppers. There was always a big bowl of creamy mashed potatoes, a chicken, baked ham or a pot roast, and lots of rich, brown gravy. She would open a jar of peas or corn or steam a mess of turnips. There would be Ma's pickles, cottage cheese, and butter to spread on bread or rolls fresh from the oven, along with a homemade pie and whipped cream. All this was topped off with big mugs of steaming coffee.

The last chore of the day was doing the night check: checking the barn and other outbuildings and lighting the oil heater in the chicken house. Then, back to the house I went for a game of checkers or cards before it was time to go up to bed.

No, life on a hill farm wasn't easy in summer or winter, but it provided us with all that we needed and more. I guess I learned at an early age that what you might want wasn't what you really needed. Yes, I miss the Good Old Days, even with all the hard work, the snow and the cold. ❖

Churning Day

By Edna P. Bates

As I picked up a pound of butter in the supermarket this week, I recalled nostalgically the delicious flavor of the butter we made from our own cows for many years.

Churning day began the night before when the can of cream was brought from the cold cellar up to the kitchen so that it would be properly sour and at room temperature. The churn was brought in from the woodshed.

When the cream was ready, scalding water was poured into the churn, over the dasher, the lid, the wooden butter bowl, ladle and "print." This was poured off and the pieces were rinsed with cold water. Then we put the sour cream in the churn, and the lid and dasher were assembled. We spread papers on the floor to catch the spatters of cream that spread as we plunged the dasher up and down. The cat liked to help out with that by licking up the spots of cream.

If the cream was the right temperature to begin with, it was soon beaten into the consistency of heavy whipped cream, and the dasher went up and down with difficulty. Then we could begin to hear splashing sounds, and it moved more easily as the butter began to form. The thick cream changed to thin, milky buttermilk, and little golden flecks of butter came up on the handle of the dasher.

Now we had to slow down and let the little bits of butter gather. When these lumps were about the size of hickory nuts, we poured the cold water out of the butter bowl and scooped the butter out of the churn with the butter ladle. To get out the last bits of butter, we could strain the buttermilk, but my dad liked some butter left in his buttermilk.

Next, we "worked" the butter with the ladle to get out all the buttermilk. Then we washed it with cold water and worked it again until no more liquid would come out. 'Twas a poor butter maker indeed who left any buttermilk in to spoil her butter!

Last we added the salt and worked it in well, draining off any liquid left.

The butter was left to "set" awhile, then it was put into "prints." These were wooden forms that held about a pound of butter. If it was to be sold, an exact pound was weighed out, then pressed firmly into the print so that no air spaces were left. Many prints had fancy patterns carved in the top. Ours just made four ridges in the top of each pound.

For special meals, we always made a few "pats" of butter. To do this, we made a ball with enough butter for the meal, then pressed it flat to fit the butter dish and made a fancy pattern on the top. These were stored carefully so as not to spoil their shape or pattern.

Making butter was fun on a good day, but if the temperature of the cream wasn't just right, or if it was during hot summer weather, it could take a lot longer. If the butter was too soft, it had to be put down in the well in a pail, or on the cellar floor till it got firm enough to work. Sometimes it took most of the day to finish the butter.

For years, my mother made butter to deliver to customers by horse and buggy, or to sell on the market 15 miles away in a nearby city. Buyers came along and tasted the butter to see which housewife's wares they liked best! My father thought "bought" butter hardly worthy of the name, and liked ours much better.

He was right, too. On churning day, we always had pancakes for supper, made with fresh buttermilk. A big square of fresh, homemade butter and brown sugar sprinkled liberally over the golden rounds hot from the pan made them food fit for the gods—or for a hungry farmer and his family! ❖

Work, Work, Work!

By Charles Stovall

When I was but a boy living on a small hillside ranch in western Oregon, never a day came but what there was work to do. I often wished for a morning when I could lie in bed until I was really ready to get up. Five o'clock came awfully early on cold, wintry mornings—but the getting up time remained the same.

Pa woke up at 4:30 and started fires in the wood range and the box heater. By the time my brother, Frank, and I reached the warmed area from our bunks upstairs, the temperature was quite comfortable. As we scampered down there carrying part of our clothes so as to don our overalls near the heater, Pa had already left for the barn, carrying the lantern.

Pa fed what livestock we had. He seemed to know just how much hay to give each animal so the supply would last through the whole winter. Since snow usually covered what little forage there might be, the cows and calves just huddled under the trees, looking discouraged, and awaited the coming of spring.

The skid road led away from the mill, up the canyon. Oxen dragged the logs down this road to the landing near the runway for the carriage.

While Pa was doing the feeding, Frank and I milked the cows. We carried the milk to the springhouse where we poured it from our large pails into shallow milk pans. These pans were placed on shelves and left for a day or more for the cream to rise and set. Each day, Ma skimmed the cream from the pans that were ready. She poured this cream into a large can that rested in the cold, spring water.

The skimmed milk was fed to the calves that had been weaned from their mothers. When the big cream can was full, or nearly so, Pa drove to town with it, taking along any butter and eggs that could be spared. He usually received enough money to buy our flour, sugar and salt. We usually drank skimmed milk, or buttermilk.

Ma had our breakfast ready at 6:30. By that time, the calves, cows, horses and hogs were finished eating. The horses and cows were let out of their stalls, or stanchions, so we could clean them, throwing the manure outside where a large pile accumulated. Before spring, we hauled it away on a sled, spreading most of it over the garden.

After the barn was cleaned, Frank and I usually worked until noon cutting wood with a crosscut saw. When Pa was not plowing or grubbing stumps, he bucked logs for a waterwheel sawmill down in a nearby canyon. The clearing and plowing were done mostly during the winter. When the worst winter weather was over, he would again resume his work at cutting logs for the mill.

One morning at the breakfast table, Pa surprised me with a new job. "Charlie," he said, "I think I will take you with me today. You sharpen your little ax and take it along. You can help by choppin' off limbs and knots on the logs. I gotta get more done down there in order to catch up on what we owe for lumber. When you get tired, you can watch the oxen drag logs down the skid row."

"Gee, Pa, that'll be a lot different for a change. I think I'll like to do that."

"And you, Frank," Pa said, "can carry water for your Ma to use in doin' the washin'! After that you can mend the picket fence around the yard. Part of it has blown over. You'll have to put in a new post, and set it deeper in the ground."

I sharpened the ax until the cutting edge looked bright and shiny. Then I went to a secret hiding place and withdrew three pieces of the hard candy I had been rationing to myself ever since Christmas. Ordinarily I ate but two pieces each day, but this day would undoubtedly be more strenuous than usual.

Ma put up a lunch for us in a 10-pound lard pail. It was my first trip to the mill where the logging was going on. I had wanted to go before this, but Pa thought I should get a little bigger and tougher, as logging was strenuous work and somewhat dangerous. I was large for a 10-year-old boy, and since I had been doing plenty of work, I guess Pa thought I would be able to help him some and not get overly tired.

The sawmill looked plenty big to me. It was interesting. Water rushed onto a great wheel and the weight of the falling water kept the big wheel turning. The constant, even rotation supplied power for the huge circular saw that buzzed and hummed as it ripped through logs, fighting every inch of the way. While the big wheel turned slowly, all the little wheels and the big circular saw revolved rapidly.

Pa took me inside the mill where I was immediately fascinated by the sight of a large log being sliced into boards. The big circular saw revolved so fast that I could not see its teeth. It hurled a steady stream of sawdust as it fought its way through the log. A carriage moved the log against the saw. The first slice was a slab that was discarded. The next slice was a rough board of the desired thickness. The saw buzzed savagely as it inched its way down the log. As each piece of lumber was sawed off, it fell over onto rollers and it was rolled away.

Then a man at each end of the log moved it the distance desired for the thickness of the next board or plank.

"Gee, Pa," I said, "I could watch this all day."

"But we must be going now to our own work. We're already late. This mill has been runnin'

nearly an hour before we cvcn get started. Come on now, we have to go up this skid road."

The skid road led away from the mill, up the canyon. A small stream ran quite close to it in many places. Oxen dragged the logs down this road to the landing near the runway for the carriage. Two men with peavies rolled logs onto the carriage as needed.

We started up the skid road, stepping high about every third step in order to get over each skid. The skids were small logs about 8 feet long, placed at regular intervals across the road for the logs to slide over. This reduced friction so they would drag easily, which they wouldn't do if they were pulled over bare ground.

In about 15 minutes we came to where branch roads without skids trailed up the canyon. "We'll go up this hillside road to where trees are being fell and bucked," said Pa, leading the way. "Two other men saw the trees down, and I buck 'em up into logs so the oxen can drag 'em out."

Pa was anxious to get started. He went up the steep hillside so fast that it was hard for me to keep up. "Pretty steep," I panted after several minutes.

"It gets better a little further up," encouraged Pa. "Anyway, we haven't much farther to go."

We soon came to a freshly felled tree. "Here we are," said Pa. "I'll leave the dinner bucket here by this big stump and we'll work on this tree. You begin choppin' off limbs and long knots that stick out so the logs will slide along easily. I'll start sawin' on this butt log. This tree will last us all day. Doubt if we get through with it even then. It will make about eight 16-foot logs."

I went to work as directed. I thought it fun for a while, chopping big limbs that cracked loudly as they broke away. Their weight was sufficient to break them loose so that I didn't have to cut much wood. However, the pleasures of such work soon wore off. The ax seemed to get heavier and heavier. Long before lunchtime, my arms began to tire. Each swing of the ax got slower and shorter.

Pa glanced my way occasionally to see how I was getting along. Noticing that I was slowing down, he stopped sawing and called to me. "Charlie, you'd better lay your ax down now and rest awhile. You can watch the oxen drag out logs to make a string of them in the skid road. Then they'll drag them down to the mill. Be careful, though, and don't get in the way. You might get hurt. When you get back, we'll eat our dinner."

"I'm not very tired, Pa, but the ax needs a rest, I guess." I really was tired, but I didn't want to admit it to Pa. I wanted him to think I was man enough to take it. I might want to go with him again sometime.

It didn't take me long to get down to the skid road where oxen had just brought in a big log and were being turned for another one. I got a thrill out of watching them maneuver.

I followed along behind them on this trip. They plodded up the hillside to where they were hooked on to another log. They dragged one log at a time until four logs were lined up in the skid road. These were "dogged" together and the oxen, eight of them yoked together in pairs, dragged the string down to the mill.

The driver of the oxen carried a goad stick for prodding the shirkers so that each team would do its share of the pulling. The goad stick was about 4 feet long and had a short,

sharp nail in one end. The driver used it more as a threat than for actual prodding, yet he let the oxen know that he would use it if they did not obey his commands.

"Buck! Bally!" he would call out. "Heave into it there!" A wave of the goad stick, and away they went, straining with their shoulders and necks to the yokes. The string of logs wound snakelike behind them.

I followed the oxen on one trip. Then I was ready to eat. I was really tired as well as hungry when I got back to where Pa was working. He spread the lunch out on a small log that we sat on while we ate. I had little more work to do that day, for which I was glad.

I made other trips with Pa, as I became stronger and more used to the work. I also learned more about skid-road logging and using oxen.

I made other trips with Pa, as I became stronger and more used to the work. I also learned more about skid-road logging and using oxen. In dry weather, one man went in advance of the oxen and "greased" the skids. Real grease, however, was not used. The road followed a creek. The "greaser" slicked the skids with water dripping from nail holes punched in the bottom of a 5-gallon kerosene can. The water slicked the skids, lessening the friction as the logs moved over them.

When I grew older and stronger, I worked at "greasing" skids. However, I soon progressed to other logging work. I enjoyed being in the woods. Many days I helped Pa when the weather was agreeable. I did a lot of the ax work, and eventually Pa bought a shorter, lighter saw for me to use. With it, I bucked the smaller trees, or the small tops of the trees Pa worked on.

Several things made timber work pleasant for me: the beauty of ferns, wildflowers and flowering shrubs, and the pure, fresh air and woodsy smell.

My young brother, Frank, did not take to the strenuous work demanded of woods workers. On the days I went with Pa, he stayed home and helped Ma some with her daily load. There was always the job of carrying water from the spring to the house. ❖

Crosscut Saw

By Lee A. Neiley

I grew up on a small dairy farm in northwestern Pennsylvania. We did not have much in the way of modern farm equipment. In my father's thinking, that was okay, as we had plenty of time to do lots of manual labor.

We did not have a chain saw, nor, in my father's mind, did we need one. Missing this labor-saving device did not keep us from cutting firewood in the winter. Oh no, not at all.

We used the crosscut saw, that device of torture used by our forefathers, to cut our firewood.

This torturous device did not use gas or oil to propel it. The cutting machine had no moving parts, except for the two unfortunate souls on the ends.

The crosscut saw was a long metal device with cutting teeth and a wooden handle on each end. One man would pull as the other man pushed. After what seemed an eternity, a tree could be cut into lengths small enough to be put onto a buzz saw (another story) to cut it into stove lengths.

Unlike the kids in town who looked forward to Saturday, I hated to see Saturday come. I knew what my fate would be. I would be in the woods with my father, on the working end of the old crosscut saw.

Hour after hour, Saturday after Saturday, there we would be, pushing and pulling that saw through the wood.

My father never did buy a chain saw. He did install an oil-burning heating unit and an electric cookstove so he no longer needed to cut wood— after I left home. ❖

A Dad Understands

By Eileen Jones McGoffin

After we retired, my brother, Curtis, and I met occasionally for lunch. Sometimes we talked of our childhood on the farm. One day he related an incident which occurred after I'd married and moved away. Here is Curtis' story as he told it to me:

It was 1940, the year before Dad got the tractor, and I was 13. I'd been working in the hayloft all day, leveling the mounds of loose hay dropped by the hayfork and spreading salt over each new layer. My back and legs ached and my arms were covered with scratches from the stiff hay stalks.

I got very thirsty, so between a couple loads, I went out to the standpipe by the watering trough in the barnyard. I was sure tired, and that afternoon sun drew more sweat and caked the dust that covered me from head to toe. My skin itched all over. Each step I took made little puffs of dust rise in that hot air.

I poured the first cup of cold water over my head, gulped down two more, then sat under the elderberry tree there, sipping more.

The men's voices floated in from the field as they loaded the wagon with hay. The horses always stood quietly, like they were grateful for the rest, until it was time to move ahead a few feet to the next group of hay shocks.

Dad stood in front of me, and I thought I'd really catch heck for goofing off.

Very soon, they would be bringing the load to the barn. The horses would be unhitched and walked to the opposite side of the barn where they were hitched to the pulley that drew the big forkfuls of hay over the loft. Each wagonload made four huge mounds of loose hay for me to spread.

Maybe this would be the last load. Then what? It would be time to do the chores—milking the cows, feeding the pigs and chickens.

I knew where I'd like to be—at the swimming hole at Cedar Creek. Probably most of the kids were already there—splashing around, cool, having fun. Probably all the kids in our little valley were already there, on a day as hot as this.

It seemed all I ever did was work. I was the last child at home, so there was no hope of ever passing these chores on to a younger brother, as the older ones had.

People said Dad was a hard worker. That seemed to be a much-admired trait in those Depression days. I'd never seen him spend

much time doing fun things except occasionally swimming. You've seen that old tennis racket and ice skates in the attic? Mom says they belonged to Dad, but I'd never seen him use them.

I was so tired, I put my head on my knees and cried. I didn't even hear the wagon come in.

Suddenly there was a hand on my shoulder. Dad stood in front of me, and I thought I'd really catch heck for goofing off—and boys weren't supposed to cry, for Pete's sake!

Dad said, "You've worked hard today, Son. Why don't you go to the creek and have a swim?"

Have a swim? I couldn't believe my ears! Take a swim, when there was still a load of hay to spread and milking to do?

"I'll manage the milking alone, this once," Dad went on.

My eyes were blurry from the tears, but they focused on Dad's hand holding out something shining. I rubbed my eyes. Car keys? Dad was offering me the keys to the family's only car? To go swimming?

Suddenly energy surged through my whole body. I jumped up. Dad was grinning. He must have been nearly 50, but maybe he did understand what it was like to have to work when you wanted to be with your buddies at the swimming hole on a blistering July afternoon. Maybe a long time ago, when he was young, he really had used that tennis racket and those skates back in Ohio.

"There hasn't been a car go by in half an hour," he said, "but drive carefully."

I'd driven only along the farm lanes, being too young for even a learner's permit. I drove very cautiously along the mile of deserted, winding, country road and arrived at the creek to the astounded stares of all the kids there.

My pals zoomed out of the water and surrounded the car. I could just see the envy oozing from them. "Your dad let you have the car? Alone? His new Ford?" Their voices rose with each question.

I sat behind the wheel and grinned. Boy, did I feel great! And at least 16.

When the hubbub started to die down, I got out and just sort of strolled over to the edge of the bridge and dove in. That cool water sure felt good, but not as good as the charge I got from driving Dad's new Ford and having the other kids see me.

My "little" brother sat smiling at this happy memory. And I was grateful for this glimpse into our family. ❖

Help From the Barnyard

Chapter Four

Work on the farm would have been impossible without the help of so many of our friends from the animal kingdom. There has never been a farm kid who didn't have his or her tale of a favorite horse, goat, cow or dog. After all, they were an important part of the farm family, these barnyard buddies of ours.

But *my* biggest lesson in the proper balance of life on the farm came not from horse, cow, dog or cat. It came from the slithery underbelly of a snake.

I, like most farm kids, had had my share of run-ins with snakes. Copperheads were pervasive; one had bitten Aunt Maude when she was in the root cellar getting jars for canning. Rattlesnakes were a bit less common, but enough had been killed around to let us know to be on guard for the rattle in the underbrush. At the creek we had to match for cottonmouths. In all those years, I had never met a snake I didn't hate. The feeling must have been the same for Mama or Daddy, because they killed every snake they came across. Or at least I thought they did.

By the time I was 11, I had grown enough to help feed the stock and milk the cows in the evening. Our farm, like so many others, no longer could support a family of five, so Daddy worked in town, 10 miles away, through the day. He handled the stock in the morning; my brother and I alternated in evening.

One summer day, as I raised the heavy lid on the grain bin, I spied a snake slithering in the corner by one of the bags. I looked quickly for something to kill it with. My memory is hazy now, but I know I found something and struck what I felt was a lethal blow. Still, in its death throes, the snake writhed and I was afraid to scoop it out of the bin, which was nearly as tall as I was. So I decided to leave it there and ask Daddy to get it out the next morning.

I forgot to mention it to Daddy that night, and missed him before he went to feed the next morning. I was at the table for breakfast when he came in the door.

"Who killed the snake in the grain bin?" Daddy asked.

"I did!" I exclaimed proudly, expecting at least a medal for bravery.

"Kenneth Tate! (I always knew I was in trouble when Daddy used my whole name.) That was a king snake! I let it stay there to keep the mice, rats and other varmits out of the grain!"

"But, Daddy!" my bravery was now reduced to sniveling. "It was a snake, and I thought we killed snakes!"

Daddy softened a bit.

"We kill snakes that threaten us," he explained. "But not all snakes are bad. Even rattlesnakes and copperheads help hold down pests. It'll take a while, but we'll get another snake to guard the grain. Just don't kill the next one without checking with me first."

He tousled my hair, then gave me a half good-natured, half serious swat on the backside—sort of like "one to grow on."

The lesson has stayed with me my entire life. My dear wife Janice hates snakes, and will periodically call me when she spies one in the garden or one of her flowerbeds. Now, don't tell her, but often as not I find out it's a harmless variety and I simply let it wriggle its way to safety. Daddy would be proud.

You'll enjoy these remembrances of those special helpers from the animal world. Whether they be snakes, horses, cows, dogs, cats—all our barnyard buddies had their place in the natural scheme of things on the farm back in the Good Old Days.

—*Ken Tate*

Real Horsepower

By Marshall Robbins

My memories of the teens and '20s of the 20th century are often more accurate than my memories of last week. A considerable number of those recollections have to do with the means of doing work in the country, and of our modes of travel.

We were past the time of oxen for farm and timber work, but horses were an absolute necessity on our Indiana farm. Our horses were neither registered nor of pedigreed stock. They were just horses of unknown breeds, or crossbreeds, but they all had names and character.

One of Dad's work animals was a mule named Jim. Speaking of characters, he was a character. His teammate was always a horse, and he usually started on command more quickly than the horse did. He would sometimes get his own pulling done before the other animal got started, then stop pulling and let the other pull alone. Of course, this was bad teamwork.

Once my dad was trying to pull a log up on a wagon with this team and was not getting good cooperation. He would never beat his horses, but would sometimes use a keen switch. After trying two or three times with no success, he cut a long switch and, standing on old Maud's side, he gave the starting command. Just as the mule was about to quit, Dad reached across the other animal's back and switched Jim on his long ears. Needless to say, the log went on the wagon; in fact, had not the other side been well propped, the log would have gone on over it.

My father worked Jim with a blind mare and had trained the mule to come out of the barn on his own. Dad would bridle Jim, then bridle the mare and lead her out to the wagon. He would call, "Come on, Jim," and the mule would walk out and come to his own side of the wagon tongue.

Once, for some reason, my father changed the order and put the mule on the opposite side of the wagon. He led the mare out from the stable and put her on Jim's side. Jim obeyed the command to come, but he went to a second wagon that Dad wasn't using that day and aligned himself on his own side. Was it that important to Jim? Or was he just giving my dad the horse (mule's) laugh?

Just as the horse furnished pulling power for wagons and farm tools,

so it also was a means of transportation, sometimes ridden, and sometimes driven when hitched to a buggy or spring wagon. And sometimes we would put hay or straw in the bottom of the bed and go where we wished in the two-horse "jolt wagon." The buggy, however, was depended on most for pleasure travel.

I went to my two older sisters' eighth-grade graduation service in a buggy. Our local blacksmith repaired and repainted buggies until they looked like new. I'm not sure they didn't even squeak like a new one. We went in this type of buggy to Andersonville, Ind., to the Christian Church where the commencement service was held. I sat on the seat with Mom and Dad and my sisters sat on a board placed across the

buggy bed, with the dashboard to lean against. That way they could protect their finery better than if they were sitting on someone's lap.

One of my chief delights as a lad of 7 was to ride to Metamora with my dad, on a load of railroad ties. We would cross the White Water River via the old covered bridge. What a clatter on its floor of thick boards. Also, we sometimes went to Riley's water mill in Metamora to get feed for stock; sometimes we might also need flour or meal for home.

My experiences with horses weren't all pleasant. Once, my brother asked me to turn his driving horse out into the pasture. I led the horse through the bars and pulled off his bridle. After unbridling him, I slapped him on the hip with my hand. That was a mistake. He reciprocated by "slapping" me in the side with one of his hoofs.

I didn't know I was badly hurt and walked over to the bars. Then I began to gasp for breath. I finally got my lungs to working, but it was about three weeks before my side felt normal.

When I was about 10, I got into the habit of grabbing the spoke of a buggy wheel when someone drove away, just for kicks or to show my strength to make the wheel slide. When two young neighbor men who had been visiting started to drive away, I took ahold of the wheel, but somehow lost my balance and fell in front of it. The man who was driving saw what was happening and said, "Whoa!" just in time to stop the buggy wheel right on my back.

I'm sure the combined weight of the two young men was considerably more than 300 pounds. I survived without much harm, but I don't remember sliding any buggy wheels thereafter.

Once, when I was a teenager, a team of horses ran away with me and threw me through a wire fence. I still have the scars from that experience, but the wires didn't cut deeply enough to do me permanent harm.

My brother drove a horse and buggy to court the lady he finally married. He usually drove an old, trusty mare named Elsie. Once he drove a younger horse named Diamond. We lived on a creek road. A freshet had washed the road out in one place, and another track was being used.

It was my brother's habit to tie the lines around the dashboard and trust the mare to take him home while he slept. He tried that with Diamond, but the young horse, being unfamiliar with the change in the road, took my sleeping brother right down over the washout. You may be sure he wasn't asleep after bumping over that bank in the buggy!

Looking back, I can't say I long for a return to the days of horse-drawn vehicles. But the events referred to here will always hang in the picture gallery of my memories. They're still vivid enough to be recalled without difficulty, a bridge, as it were, to interesting yesteryears. ❖

The Old Barn

By Carlton C. Buck

Tell me, old horse, how old is this barn?

It seems to have weathered many a storm.

The hinges are rusted, the shingles are loose,

And the creaky old hayloft has seen plenty of use.

The swallows have nested for many years?

And what of the milkmaids, their laughter and tears?

I am sure there are stories of romance and pain,

Of hard winter storms with snow, wind and rain.

Was there a young farmer when the barn was brand new,

Who brought his young bride and escorted her through?

Did they have many children who played in the hay

And brought in the cows at the close of each day?

Did the family grow old as the old barn has done,

And leave the old farm at life's setting sun?

Did the young folk all leave and move off to town?

Was the old barn deserted until at last it falls down?

Tell me, old horse, if your father told you,

Of the romance and pathos since the old barn was new.

Golden

By Harold Williams

That leathery razorback was out for blood—mine.

When I was 6, pneumonia paid a fatal visit to my mother and father and left me an orphan. My grandparents took me in and I spent my childhood on their farm.

In those days, my grandparents were my sole companions—well, almost. There was one other. That was Grandpa's dog.

The old man called him Golden, and no other name could have fit as well. His sleek coat glowed under the sun and looked just like that precious metal. A big dog, Golden moved with the pride and grace of a giant timberwolf.

My grandfather, Lucius, had owned him from a pup and he was nothing else but Lucius' dog. He'd romp and play with me, but if Lucius appeared, Golden would stop and stare silently at his master, waiting for a command, poised for instant obedience.

Lucius had trained him for a cattle dog and the old man swore he'd never seen a better one. I'd watch them coming home at sunset, bringing a great herd of cattle, and the cows would be so tightly bunched you'd think they had a rope around them.

The old man would walk off to one side and his dog would drift right and left behind the herd, keeping them moving, keeping them controlled. Occasionally a cow would break off and go scampering to one side and I'd hear the old man yell, "Hah, Golden!" and point to the offender. But by then a flash of amber had appeared on the other side of the animal and brought her back into line.

Rufus Steinbeck, a neighboring farmer, ached to own the dog and asked Lucius to name his price.

"He can't be bought at any price," muttered Grandpa, walking away.

"That your final decision?" Rufus called after him.

"It is," said the old man over his shoulder.

That decision saved my life.

For years, wild hogs had roamed the hills and gorges of Crowley's Ridge. These creatures were truly feral, with lean bodies and elongated snouts. Curved, sharp tusks protruded from their lower jaw. They could disembowel a much larger animal with one vicious swipe. Always hostile, they would attack without provocation. They feared man not at all.

I could hear our three sows squealing in terror. I ran as I had never run before, but I knew it was hopeless.

One Saturday morning I finished breakfast and asked Grandpa if I could go down to Bear Creek and fish off the bank. He said yes, but first I needed to carry some water to the hogs. I went out to the pump with a metal pail in each hand. I filled the small buckets, then carried them over to the hog pen. I was about to open the gate when I heard a bang and the splintering of wood. Whatever made the sound was outside the fence and around the corner.

Slowly, with hammering heart, I started forward, still clutching the pails of water in my hands. I reached the corner and stepped around it.

The huge wild boar was busy trying to break through the fence. He thrust his fierce, ugly snout under the bottom railing and jerked it upward, causing the pine wood to split and fly apart. Dingy tusks rose from both sides of his bottom jaw and ended in sharp points just above the flared nostrils. He was looking into the pen, but suddenly he swung his head around and both inflamed eyes were boring into me.

Instantly, he lowered that head and charged.

For a split-second I stood transfixed. Then I dropped the pails and ran for the house. I heard a clang behind me and glanced back to see one of the pails sailing end over end, water spraying from it in a glistening fan. The boar had slowed for a moment to hit the pail, but now he was on me again.

He never made a sound, but I could hear our three sows squealing in terror. I ran as I had never run before, but I knew it was hopeless. He was too fast for me. I could hear him right behind me and I felt his hot breath on my bare ankles. Suddenly, a flash of pain ripped across the back of my leg as he slashed me with a tusk. I screamed and tried to run faster and looked ahead in bug-eyed terror at the home I would never reach.

Then it happened. My grandfather appeared on the front porch, followed by a dog that couldn't be bought at any price. He stared at the scene before him, then stretched out his long right arm like an avenging prophet, at the monster behind me. And his voice sounded as a bugle in the face of my fear.

"Haaaahhhh, Golden!"

The great dog bounded up and sprang off the porch. He sailed through the air and then he was on the ground and coming like a tawny streak. I saw that broad head, with the ears laid back and the white fangs bared and I heard the rumbling growl come from deep in his throat. As my grandpa's dog rose once more into the air, I thought for a fearful moment that he had come for me.

I screamed and threw myself forward and felt the wind from Golden's passing. Behind me, I heard the whump of bodies colliding and the shrill cry of the boar. My lips twitched in a smile before I passed out, because what had come from the boar was a squeal of pain.

Later that morning, I awoke with some pain of my own. Grandpa had laid me on the couch and Grandma was holding a cup of hot tea under my nose. The pain came from my leg and I looked down to see it wrapped in a bandage.

"You're all right," she said, handing the cup to Grandpa and placing a cool palm on my forehead. "The cut wasn't deep. I put some disinfectant on it, but you keep that bandage on for a while."

She went back into the kitchen and Grandpa held the tea to my lips. I took a deep swallow and felt the warm liquid go all the way to my stomach.

Grandpa smiled and said, "You had a close call." Then, assuming his black-eyed, grim look, he murmured, "I called the dog off and the boar ran away. Maybe I'll meet him again sometime."

I stared up at him and asked, "Grandpa, where is he?"

"Why, right here," said the old man as he got up and opened the front door. Morning sunlight streamed through the doorway, lighting a golden presence in the center. Grandpa's dog padded into the room and stood by the couch, looking at me. I threw both arms around him and buried my face in his neck and kept it there for a long time, while sob after sob racked my body.

Finally, I sank back down on the couch. The great dog remained motionless at my side. Seeing the questioning look in his eyes, I slowly nodded my head. Then, Golden turned and trotted through the door, following his master who'd gone out before him. ❖

Big Joe: Long May He Wave!

By Rugh M. Dirgo

Every pioneer farm family has at least one snake story, and my in-laws are no exception. But Paw, being the type to embroider everything he told, had several. The one we laughed most about was Big Joe.

Big Joe was a sizable old blacksnake (I think!) who had lived on the farm so long he had squatter's rights. Grampa said he more than earned his keep by keeping the rodent population down, and by strict orders, Joe was never interfered with.

The story I am about to tell happened during the time Uncle Hank and Aunt Tillie lived on the old place. Down the road a piece were another old couple, Herb and Annie. Annie and Tillie had been friends for years, and it was their custom to spend a day with each other now and then, sewing carpet rags, piecing quilts and so forth. For some reason, Annie had never met up with Joe.

One lovely day, Annie came over for the usual visit, and during the course of the afternoon, she made a routine trip to the "necessary" house. This was a classy little number with a crescent moon on two sides, and a little corner shelf for the Sears-Roebuck catalog. Annie arranged herself comfortably for a few minutes of cogitation (probably long enough for Tillie to finish the dinner dishes). All this time, she had not noticed Big Joe, who was hanging from the rafter.

Now what his thoughts were, we shall never know. Maybe, since she had not hollered and run, he figured she was not against being friendly. He lowered himself and swayed, but with her nose buried in the "wish book," she did not notice, so Joe let go and landed with a nice plop! right smack in her lap. Tillie swore that Hank heard Annie's screams clear back on the north 40. Poor old Joe was so scared he didn't show up for a week. Hank always vowed that Annie had to borrow Tillie's underwear to wear home, which Tillie would never confirm nor deny, only saying, "Now, Hank, the poor thing was skeered, and you woulda been, too!"

My daughter met Big Joe when she was climbing into the haymow to hunt eggs. About halfway up the ladder, she became aware of something like the pendulum on a grandfather clock, swaying to and fro. Her husband commented that he had been figuring on putting an extra door in the side of the barn for quite a spell. Kate—with Big Joe's help—just hurried things up a little bit. ❖

Joey, Jake & Dad

By Peter R. Koens

When my mother went to a retirement home, I became the custodian of the family photo album and the family Bible. Simple possession allows me to be the keeper of the family legend and its rich history.

Every once in a while I look at the snapshots, especially the faded sepia pictures, and then I wish I could cross through the veil of space and time and talk with my ancestors.

In any case, now I have faces to attach to the signatures in our old, old Bible. The colors of the ink are like the pictures—sun-faded browns, cracked blacks and illegible blues.

Surprisingly, I found a photograph taped inside, covering St. Luke, Chapter 7—a tinted photo of my father with two horses, obviously on a farm. It came as a bit of a surprise.

I had never known that Dad had owned horses or had worked on a farm. I was curious and wanted to get to the bottom of the story. A week or so later, when I went to the retirement home to visit my mother, I took the picture with me.

I showed her the picture and she gasped. She took the snapshot and stroked the picture as if it were alive, whispering, "Oh, Joey, Joey! Oh, you beautiful boy!"

Dad was good with animals. He treated them well and cared for them and they responded by working well. That spring he was able to start farming.

I was surprised, to say the least. "Who is Joey?" I asked. She turned to me and it seemed that a veil had been lifted from her eyes. They sparkled and she seemed at least 50 years younger. She began to talk, and her voice held the timbre and vibrancy of a 20-year-old.

"Your father came back from Canada in 1934. I met him at a dance and we fell in love. We got engaged secretly and we were going to be married in Canada after we had the farm he wanted."

"What farm?" I asked. She recounted how she had sold her life insurance policies and traded in some bonds and Dad worked overtime to make the down payment. When all was said and done, they ended up with enough money to pay cash for the right property.

Dad took the money and returned to southern Ontario to find the farm which would become home to their dreams. Instead, it became a crucible, testing their strengths, values and beliefs, and finally their marriage.

He bought their farm and bought into the Great Depression. He equipped it with fire-sale items from neighbors who were selling out, moving to town or the nearest city to get a job and make cash money. Usually they ended up "on the dole."

He bought two horses, Joey and Jake, from a neighbor who was leaving to look for his long-overdue sons trekking somewhere through the network of American Hoovervilles.

The horses were in rough shape. He got the two of them for $16 and their harness for $12, but he balked at paying $2.50 for blinders. He took them to his place and on the road back he found out Jake was miserable—a kicker and biter. Joey had been maimed; he was a very quiet 6-year-old stallion.

Dad was good with animals. He treated them well and cared for them and they responded by working well. That spring he was able to start farming.

In the meantime, Mom had set a date for their wedding and was crossing the ocean on the Holland-America line's ship Staatendam. She traveled from New York on the Penn Central line to Windsor and arrived a good half-hour before the ceremony was to start.

Nine months later, she gave birth to a lovely 7-pound baby girl. The Depression had worsened. Factories shut, down and young fellows rode the rails looking for nonexistent work. Offices closed. Both Canada and the United States seemed to be at a standstill.

They had had a Model-T Ford, but it had

This is the photograph I found in the family Bible. In it, Dad stands with Joey while Jake grazes in the background.

given up the ghost and they couldn't replace it. Neighbors had taken them into town to see a movie, *Rosemarie*, with Jeannette MacDonald and Nelson Eddy. Afterward, they spent their last quarter in a hamburger joint, and while they shared a banana split, they heard a new song, *My Baby Just Cares for Me*, on the jukebox.

It was a good song, Mom said, because that's all a lot of people had left—a solid marriage. During that terrible decade, even the weather didn't help. One year the crops burned, the next year they were flooded. The land dried out and the winds blew topsoil into the next county. This was their third year and they had to make it. They were broke.

Even though they had been in town and had talked about the movie and the songs they had heard until the early morning, Dad was up and plowing at 5 o'clock. He had a small contract with Heinz for his tomato crop and he was planting 50 acres. Defeat and failure tire a man and, because of the past two years, he was bone tired, burned out before his time.

He was working with a cultivator; Joey and Jake were pulling. Mom decided she would make a picnic-style lunch and, just like in the movies, take the little girl with her to the bottom of the farm so they could all have lunch together.

She left just before noon. The sky had turned an ugly lemon topped with dark clouds. The wind died down and it became cooler. Then lightning began to ripple across that eerie sky. Electricity crackled, ozone burned and a nervous Jake lashed out with his hind legs and kicked Joey hard. He turned in his traces, and before he could move, Dad was on his back, the spiked blades lodged on his leg and shoulder.

Mom saw the situation, but she was still more than 100 yards away. Lightning slashed across the skies again, and in this witch's cauldron, Jake went crazy with fear. Joey strained to keep his partner on track. Jake swung about to try another kick, but Joey lunged and bit him hard on the shoulder. The shock and pain settled Jake down.

Mom had run hard, leaving Mary behind to fend for herself, as she lived out the reality of *My Baby Just Cares for Me* and got the horses under control. Dad was able to get up with nothing worse than hurt pride.

Mom had run the race against death again in her memory, and, at 90, she was exhausted. Simply telling me the story had sapped her strength.

I was about to leave when I turned and asked, "How in God's name did Dad train Joey to stand still during a lightning storm?"

"He didn't have to," she said. "I told you the horse was maimed; I forgot to tell you Joey was blind." ❖

A Horse Like Nell

By J.B. Cearley

*I*t was during my 14th summer, when I was farmed out to work for my Uncle Oran, that I became acquainted with Nell, a wonderful old gray mare.

Early Monday morning, I got up and dressed for a day in Uncle's field. When I walked into the kitchen, the satisfying aroma of bacon, scrambled eggs and hot biscuits floated to my nostrils. There was also cereal, and jam galore.

Uncle Oran Cearley glanced at me as he said, "Better sit and eat a spell before we hit the field." he took his place at the table. When Auntie sat, Uncle prayed, thanking God for the food and asking for a little rain. It was usually dry in West Texas.

This was my first introduction to my aunt and uncle. They were a friendly, caring old couple, and Uncle was a unique person. I observed this while we were eating breakfast. He was jolly and contented as he buttered his biscuits and cleaned up his eggs and bacon. But it was the bowl of cereal he ate that told me he was an individualist. He poured a bowl of cornflakes, added a handful of raisins, a spoonful of sugar, milk, and topped it off with some pure cream from the separator. He laughed at me, a skinny kid staring at him from across the table. "Man has to eat to work," he told me.

A few minutes later, we walked out to the cattle corral and prepared to hit the fields.

"You'll run the sled go-devil with Nell and Judd," he said. "Be gentle and easy with Nell because she is a little blind and 11, but she's a queen of a horse."

I walked out to her in the big corral, carrying the bridle. After I spoke gently, she pricked up her ears and turned to look toward me. I petted her neck and back, then slipped the bridle on and led her to the harness rack. Harnessing Nell was easy. When I went to catch Judd, her plow mate, that was a different story; Judd was a little wild, mean, quick to bite a kid, and anxious to run away. After I had chased him around the corral three times, Uncle Oran hit him with a small rock, gave him a tongue-lashing, and took a rope to him. Judd eventually let us harness him with great reluctance.

I fastened the reins to each horse's bridle and was ready for the field. Uncle Oran had a four-horse hitch to pull a two-row go-devil, which had wheels. The one-row go-devil I was to ride was made out of two 2-by-10 boards, 3 feet long, with a metal runner on the bottom. It had two long knives to cut the weeds from the middle. Two small plows cut weeds and threw dirt to the crops. A metal seat was mounted above the boards that were 10 inches apart to straddle the crop.

She was a once-in-a-lifetime experience. Harnessing Nell was easy. When I went to catch Judd, her plow mate, that was a different story.

Nell was gentle and easy to hitch to the doubletree, but old Judd decided he would be contrary. Uncle Oran got tired of Judd's behavior and slammed his number 10 brogan into Judd's ribcage. Then the ornery horse was content to be hitched to the plow.

Uncle turned to say, "Watch that crazy horse. I think Nell will keep him from causing trouble. Take it easy with Nell." While she didn't look like much, I figured Nell was something special.

I drove out to the small grain field I was to plow and turned onto a row. The horses were supposed to walk on a small mound of dirt between the rows. Almost-blind Nell took her place like a trained circus animal. Judd, on the other hand, wanted to swing wide and walk in the next furrow, his ponderous feet trampling the crop. I yelled at him, trying to scare him into walking in the proper place. After he kept disobeying my command, I hit him with the ends of the leather reins. Then he wanted to run away. I noticed that Nell kept turning toward him as if she were trying to get him to walk in the correct place.

It was driving Nell and me a little goofy as we struggled with Judd. After an hour of work, Nell had had enough of Judd's foolishness. She turned, opened her mouth wide and clamped it down on top of old Judd's neck. He let out a yell of protest. After that, Judd stayed in his proper place for an hour as the little sled go-devil slipped along the row.

Eventually, Judd grew lazy and mean again. I coaxed and pleaded, but he would not mind. Nell suddenly whirled in the harness and slammed her feet into Judd's belly. He almost went down. I was both surprised and pleased. After that, Judd stayed in his proper place for the rest of the morning.

I had let Nell set her own pace because Uncle said she was old and could tire. I wondered if Uncle might feel I had not covered enough land. When he stopped at noon, I noticed he drove slowly past where I had plowed, looking to see how I had done. I was a little worried. Then he said, "Looks real good, Son. Let's go eat."

We took the horses to the corral so they could get water, eat some grain and hay, and rest for an hour. Uncle and I had his usual noon meal: roast beef, green beans, corn, scalloped potatoes, sliced tomatoes, iced tea and hot biscuits. Auntie was a real cook, one from the old school.

After lunch and some rest, we returned to the field. The horses did fine for two hours. Then, contrary Judd began acting up. Nell had put up with Judd's foolishness long enough; now she was mad. She bit across the top of his head, making his right ear bleed. He decided to do right the rest of the day.

After we returned to the corral, I removed the harness and Nell trotted to her favorite place to lie down and roll around. Then she was ready for the feed trough. A horse was in her place, so Nell gently nudged the horse. When the horse did not move, Nell bit him. Uncle saw the action and laughed. "Nell is the boss here," he said. "If they get her favorite place, she can make them move. That's quite a horse, that Nell."

I began to realize why he and Auntie felt so kindly about Nell. She was just an average-looking gray horse, weighing 1,000 pounds, but she had a special personality that made her a wonder. She was never any trouble, unlike the other horses and mules.

By the time Saturday afternoon arrived and my folks came for me, I had become familiar with all the stock. But I had begun to love that old gray mare.

Fall came and I started back to school. But 10 days before Christmas, Uncle Oran asked if I could work the week I was out of school. My folks said yes, and I could use the $1.50 a day he paid. Most folks only paid $1 or $1.25 a day.

I noticed that Nell was in the big corral while the other horses were in the 10-acre pasture. I asked Uncle why and he said, "Nell is almost blind now. I don't want her to get cut on the barbed-wire fence."

It was true. Nell was almost completely blind. We worked her some, but it was obvious that she could not see well.

I was petting Nell one evening when Uncle said, "She's still the boss. Nell likes to work and she is the best horse on the place. Pretty soon she can retire and just live her in the corral where she has feed and water."

On Christmas Eve, Uncle had us quit work at noon. "It's time to think about Christmas, Son," he told me. After supper that night, I got a real surprise. Uncle was sitting at the table when he said, "I know Nell will tell all the other livestock that it's Christmas. She is the only one who would understand."

Then he reached for a book, opened it and began to read a poem by Thomas Hardy. I listened to his strong voice as he read:

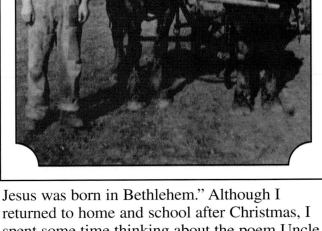

The Oxen

Christmas Eve, and 12 of the clock.
"Now they are all on their knees,"
An elder said as we sat in a flock
by the embers in hearthside ease.
We pictured the meek, mild creatures where
They dwelt in their strawy pen,
Nor did it occur to one of us then
To doubt they were kneeling there.
So fair a fancy few would weave
In these years! Yet, I feel
If someone said on Christmas Eve,
"Come see the oxen kneel.
In a lonely barton by yonder coomb
Our childhood used to know,"
I should go with him in the gloom,
Hoping it might be so.

Uncle turned to me and said, "Christmas is a blessed time of the year. It is the time when Jesus was born in Bethlehem." Although I returned to home and school after Christmas, I spent some time thinking about the poem Uncle had read to me.

When another summer came, I was again asked to work for my old uncle, now bent by arthritis in his back. Though Nell could see very little, we used her some when necessary. The old girl was still stout and willing to work. I noticed Uncle Oran had bought a large pail of stock syrup, and he poured some of it over Nell's special feed.

Another year passed, and the blind mare was left to her ease, having the run of the corral. She could smell the water trough and the feed, so she had plenty to eat in her retirement, especially since Uncle had traded all of his other horses for a John Deere farm tractor. But he and Auntie would never think of parting with dear, gentle, blind Nell.

The year I finished high school, Nell passed away. When I visited my uncle, I walked down to the back of the pasture and stood for a while looking at her grave. She had loved us, worked with us and did her share. She seemed almost human. No mere machine could ever replace a faithful plowhorse like that. She was some horse, that Nell. ❖

A Cat to Remember

By Doris C. Crandall

*I*n the Dust Bowl days of the 1930s, many of our neighbors gave up trying to make a living from the topsoil-less land in the Texas Panhandle. Just like the families in John Steinbeck's book, *The Grapes of Wrath*, they loaded meager belongings into old cars and trucks and headed for California. Our friends couldn't take everything they owned, and one family left their white Persian cat with us.

We really didn't need a cat—anyway, not that kind of cat. We already had seven regular, hardworking, no-favors-asked farm cats. "That cat won't fit in," I said to Mama.

"Shush," she replied. "We're lucky. The Everest family left their grandpa with the Petersons. 'Too old to make the journey,' they said."

Well, I thought, better a cat than a grandpa. At least the cat can stay outside.

Wrong! The new cat prissed into our house on her little furry feet, pranced around in front of everybody and showed off fit to strangle. She looked at me with her one blue eye and one green eye and said "Meow" in the softest cat voice I'd ever heard. But she didn't melt my hard-hearted resolve. I put her outside. We had never allowed our farm cats inside the house, and Queenie would just have to cope the best way she could.

Mrs. Cunning didn't like to catch mice. She preferred to lounge on a pillow and have meals brought in.

I changed her name to Mrs. Cunning. Queenie sounded like royalty, and we didn't tolerate supremacy. We treated each cat the same and each had to catch its share of mice.

Mrs. Cunning didn't like to catch mice. She preferred to lounge on a pillow and have meals brought in. Would she line up with the other cats and catch the milk Daddy squirted straight from the cows as he milked? Never! She insisted on having her milk in a saucer, and she drank it with one dainty paw steadying the bowl. She reminded us of a society lady drinking tea with her pinkie stuck straight out.

Her uppity ways riled us so much we began to call her "that cat." She even irked the farm cats, and they wouldn't so much as meow at her.

That cat sneaked into the house every chance she got. We locked her out at night, but she outsmarted us. She climbed on top of the house, scratched a hole in the window screen, and came in through an

open upstairs window. I nearly had a "catniption" fit the night she awakened me purring around my face.

She had another cute trick up her ruff, too. When she thought she wasn't getting the attention due, she sprang it on me. I was hanging the freshly washed clothes on the line in rhythm to my humming *When the Roll is Called Up Yonder.* Mrs. Cunning was the furthest thing from my mind. She slunk up behind me, sprang onto my back and dug in. I thought I'd been struck by a chicken hawk. I screamed and dropped Daddy's long johns in the dirt.

I made a grab for her. "I'll send you to your roll call right here and now!" I screeched. She dashed off with her tail high in the air.

Then, one day, a short-haired, bluish-gray tomcat, handsome in the Rhett Butler style, showed up at our farm. The gay, devilish fellow ignored the young farm females and went after Mrs. Cunning. He got her, and then the scoundrel ran off. We never saw him again.

We couldn't blame Mrs. Cunning; she'd led a sheltered life and probably didn't know any better. Maybe she had fallen in love. We pitied her. She had to raise her litter of short-haired, multicolored kittens all alone.

After that, Mrs. Cunning gave up her foolish, high-hat ways and began to act like we thought a farm cat should. She learned to catch mice with the best of the cats, seldom tried to get into the house, and never again sprang on my back.

Mrs. Cunning's efforts to fit in with the bunch endeared her to me and my family and to the other cats as well. We learned to love her. It became clear that changing her name didn't alter the fact that she really was a queen.

Over the years, all the other cats we reared on our farm blended into one big blur in my mind—all but Queenie. Now there was a cat to remember. ❖

Yetta, The Giver

By Muriel J. Titus

Yetta was our family cow when I was growing up on a little farm in Iowa. Grandma found the name in her book of names; it meant "the giver."

She said a giver was what we wanted in a family cow. Pa said Yetta was a giver, all right—she gave him more trouble than any cow he had ever owned.

Because of her inquisitive nature and the problems it caused, Yetta had to be the best of our cows to keep her big ears, shiny black nose and huge brown eyes out of the local sale barn. I'm sure, however, that if she had ended up there, it would have been just another adventure to her.

Our cows were basically black and so was Yetta. She was bigger and heavier and shinier than most. Best of all, she had the biggest, shiniest calf every year.

Every time she would crawl through the fence to eat from the side ditches, or visit the cornfield to chomp off a few tender ears, or trample the vegetable garden at home or at the neighbors', there would be a family discussion about getting rid of Yetta. But one glimpse at her current calf, or her daughters, who were always kept for replacements in the herd, and the discussion was over. Yetta had been born on this farm and would die on this farm.

Yetta got into trouble mostly because she was just plain nosy. She was always getting cussed out for dumping boxes of nuts and bolts, buckets of oats or containers of hydraulic fluid or oil.

Yetta got into trouble mostly because she was just plain nosy. If I walked or drove the pickup across the pasture, she was trailing right behind to see what I might be carrying or where I was going.

If a truck stopped long enough, Yetta would stretch her long neck over the side, even raising her front feet off the ground, to investigate the contents of the pickup bed. She was always getting cussed out for dumping boxes of nuts and bolts, buckets of oats or containers of hydraulic fluid or oil. It was especially bad if she mixed the contents, which she frequently did.

One summer, Pa decided we needed to give the barn a new coat of white paint. It wasn't very long before Yetta was walking around the pasture with a white stripe across her black face. The painter claimed she was trying to push the ladder over with him on it just to see what he had in the bucket.

His only defense, he claimed, was to hit her with the paintbrush while holding on to the ladder for dear life with his other hand. Pa had to promise to keep Yetta shut out of the barn lot before the painter would finish the job, and Yetta had a white stripe on her nose for several months.

Yetta taught my brothers and me a good lesson about keeping gates closed. One evening we left the pasture gate unchained, thinking we would be right back. Of course, we were distracted and forgot all about it. The next morning, a very angry neighbor woke us driving Yetta and her big bull calf home.

It seems she had trampled and eaten most of the sweet corn crop that was supposed to help feed his large family during the coming winter.

As Pa drove Yetta and her calf into the barn lot, our mother tried to soothe the irate neighbor by promising him our whole sweet corn crop, picked and delivered to his door by the forgetful trio who left the gate unchained.

I don't know about my brothers, but I always remember the winter we went without corn on the menu, thanks to Yetta. Also, it seems I occasionally get the urge for a roasting ear when I'm chaining a gate around the farm.

Yetta was forever getting loose, and she seldom needed any help from us. One summer our grandparents came to stay with us while our folks took a rare vacation.

Grandpa was sure a two-legged animal could outsmart a four-legged animal, and Yetta was going to learn to stay at home. He made a yoke from the fork of a tree branch and wired it to Yetta's neck. She snorted and shook her head, but walked around for three days with the large

wooden Y attached to her neck. On the fourth day, she was gone.

We searched everywhere and called around to the neighbors. No one had seen her, and we grew concerned about what Pa would say when he returned. Grandpa claimed to not be worried. He said it was good riddance that she was gone. He was just sorry she'd taken a nice calf with her. He said he wasn't worried—but he spent a lot of time tramping through the woods and checking for holes in the pasture fence.

On the day our parents arrived home, my brothers and I rushed to tell them what Grandpa had done to Yetta to make her run away for good.

Much to our surprise, Pa just took off his cap and slapped it on his leg as he laughed. "That would have been a really good joke on me if I hadn't seen Yetta and her calf grazing in the pasture as we drove up the lane."

We could hardly believe it. Grandpa looked much relieved. Yetta was home again, but she no longer wore her wooden yoke.

Yetta lived to be 19 years old. She continued to give us beautiful calves—and problems—to the end. Pa never quit cussing at her, but he knew in his heart that she was an old friend who contributed to the prosperity of our farm and our lives. For years after Yetta died, we still blamed spilled buckets, broken-down fences, open gates and other mishaps on her ghost. ❖

William

By Georgia A. Ellis

Many years ago, I lived with my mother and stepfather and five brothers and sisters on a small piece of ground at the edge of Elwood. We didn't have a lot of material things and we all had chores to do. Feeding hogs and chickens, hoeing in the garden, canning and quilting were just part of every day. We still found time to play, and we had a wonderful time.

My stepfather bought us a large, cantankerous billy goat, which we kids promptly christened William Tell. His primary function was to be a portable lawn mower, but to us, he was a pet. We lavished him with affection and brushing, and he behaved like a puppy on most occasions.

Then it was decided he could further earn his keep if he could pull a cart. This was quite an adventure for us since we didn't have a pony. We felt sure William could do the job. He had other ideas, however. The beautiful red cart being brought out was a signal for William to change to a bucking bronco.

At last he accepted the inevitable and pulled us around the yard and down the road to pick up mail. My older brother, Charles, decided to make some extra money, so he piled vegetables from our garden in the cart and William pulled it around as he sold them. It wasn't always easy, for more than once William leaped stiff-legged up in the air and dumped everything.

Looking back, William is among some of the fonder memories I have of a happy childhood, when children made their own fun without expensive toys or a television set. I wrote little verse in memory of my long-ago friend. ❖

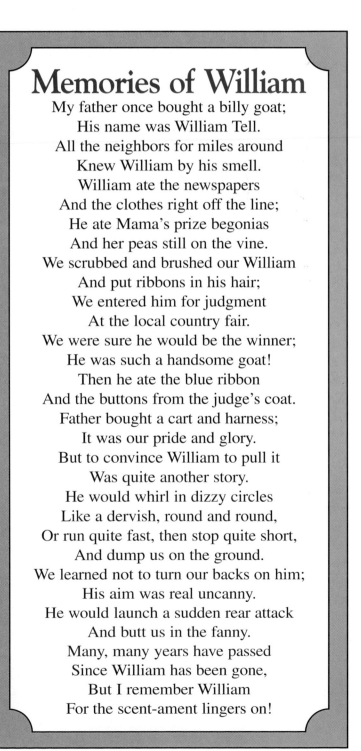

Memories of William

My father once bought a billy goat;
His name was William Tell.
All the neighbors for miles around
Knew William by his smell.
William ate the newspapers
And the clothes right off the line;
He ate Mama's prize begonias
And her peas still on the vine.
We scrubbed and brushed our William
And put ribbons in his hair;
We entered him for judgment
At the local country fair.
We were sure he would be the winner;
He was such a handsome goat!
Then he ate the blue ribbon
And the buttons from the judge's coat.
Father bought a cart and harness;
It was our pride and glory.
But to convince William to pull it
Was quite another story.
He would whirl in dizzy circles
Like a dervish, round and round,
Or run quite fast, then stop quite short,
And dump us on the ground.
We learned not to turn our backs on him;
His aim was real uncanny.
He would launch a sudden rear attack
And butt us in the fanny.
Many, many years have passed
Since William has been gone,
But I remember William
For the scent-ament lingers on!

Ruffled Feathers

By Helen Luecke

He strutted around the chicken pen like he owned it. His golden feathers and red comb glistened in the bright Texas sun. I didn't like him. In all of my eight years, this was the first creature I immediately disliked.

"Sarge is his name," Daddy said. "A bantam rooster, just what we need. With our seven little hens, it won't be long before we'll have us a bunch of chicks."

"He's going to kill all our hens!" I yelled as he chased Bitsy, my pet hen, and pecked her on the head. "You ought to take him back while you can."

Daddy smiled, gave my braids a playful tug and went inside.

Mama, Daddy and my sister, Babs, thought Sarge was cute. He still seemed mean and sneaky to me. Two days later, I went inside the pen to gather eggs. Halfway to the henhouse, Sarge charged me. I barely made it to the safety of the building. I slammed the door and hollered as loud as I could, "Somebody better get out here quick before I kill that crazy rooster!"

Sarge posted himself at the door and wouldn't budge. Mama came and shooed him away. He didn't bother her; he seemed to like her.

In the following weeks, I watched Babs, Mama and Daddy go in and out of the chicken pen. They were friends with Sarge. But let me set foot inside the gate and the war began.

I loved my pet chickens. Sarge, the bantam rooster, loved them, too. A war between us was inevitable.

"It's because you and Sarge are so much alike that you don't get along," Babs said. "He wants to rule the yard and then here you come, petting Bitsy, feeding her out of your hand and playing around with the other hens."

"That's too bad. They were my chickens first. I don't bother him, and he had darn well better leave me alone or he'll be sorry."

I stayed away from the chicken yard for a few weeks. One evening I saw Sarge at the other end of the pen, so I went in to pet and feed Bitsy. After all, I had raised her from a fluffy little chick.

I turned over a box and sat down. Bitsy jumped up and pecked lightly on my hand. I rubbed her smooth feathers and held out some grain. She clucked. I laughed.

Loud cackling and flapping wings caused me to turn around just in time to see Sarge sailing through the air, straight in my direction. I screamed, Bitsy flew, and Sarge flogged. His sharp spurs dug into my arms, legs, back, anywhere he could hit. I was a bloody mess by the time Daddy separated us.

After I got out of the bathtub, Mama put iodine on my battle wounds. "Blow it! Blow it!" I screamed, jumping around the room. "This is all that old banty's fault!"

"Take a stick in the pen with you and don't ever turn your back on him." She held me by my scratched arms and blew lightly on the open cuts.

"He's trying to kill me and all the hens, but Daddy still keeps him. Why?" She shook her head and walked to the kitchen.

Babs thought it was amusing. "I don't know what to think of you, Cozy, letting a little old rooster get the best of you. Boy, I bet that was funny!"

"Just you wait! The fight's not over yet," I said, holding back tears. "That old rooster ain't seen the last of me."

The following Saturday, I watched Mama kill some hens. That meant chicken and dumplings for Sunday dinner. She took the hen by the neck and swung it briskly around in front of her. Finally the head came off, leaving the body to flop on the ground. My plan began to take shape.

Each morning, Daddy took a pail of grain to the chickens. He scattered it around, then filled three metal feeders. I watched for a couple of days to see exactly what Sarge did during breakfast. The timing must be perfect.

One cool October morning, I followed Daddy to the open pen. I watched him do his chores and then my eyes settled on Sarge. Quietly I entered the gate, tiptoed up behind Sarge and grabbed him by the neck. With all my strength, I swung him around and around, windmill style. It was

harder than I thought. He flapped his wings and tried to get away. His feet hit the ground with each downward swing. I hung on and swung faster, my arm aching. By this time, Daddy had heard the commotion and came running.

"Cozy! Put Sarge down, now!"

I tried to give him one more swing, but Daddy stopped me. "Have you gone crazy? What are you doing?"

"Trying to kill him, that's what!"

Daddy carefully looked Sarge over to see if he was hurt. When Daddy stood him up, he wobbled, then fell, his neck held oddly to one side. Slowly he got up, fluffed his feathers, and walked around.

Darn, I whispered to myself. He's tougher than I thought. I headed for the house, dreading the scolding I knew was coming.

Babs met me at the back door. "Cozy, what have you done now? I can tell by your face. What is it?"

"I tried to kill Sarge," I said. "I tried to wring his mean old neck."

"You what? Boy, is Daddy going to be mad. Here he comes now," she said, looking out the back window. "Well, I hate to tell you this, but Sarge got the best of you again."

I could hear her laughing as she walked down the hall to her room. Tears welled up in my eyes.

Daddy came in and sat down. Calmly, he spoke to me. "Cozy, you and Sarge must learn to get along. We have to have him so we can have little chicks. Take a stick when you go inside the pen. But remember, no neck wringing, okay?"

"Okay," I said, nodding my head. Daddy patted my shoulder and handed me a stick of Juicy Fruit gum, my favorite.

From that day on, Sarge never came around me again. We seemed to have formed a mutual understanding. ❖

Black Pup

By William McGaughey

A farm in the hills of Nebraska in the 1920s and 1930s was a lonely spot. As a boy growing up in the area, I sometimes went for weeks without seeing neighbors scattered over the sparsely settled community. Although each farm had a dog, occasionally a female dog would mate with a coyote and live with him. Coyote dens were plentiful and close by. One of our neighbors had a collie that lived with a coyote in a den and had a litter of pups. This is the story of one of those pups.

Dad and the neighbor brought the pups and their mother home from the den that had been dug into a clay bank under a cedar tree. There were five pups in the litter, three males and two females. We asked for the smallest of the males. He was coal black except for a white heart-shaped spot on his chest about the size of the flat of your hand. He became Black Pup, and the name remained with him all of his life. He was a feisty little whelp and he had teeth as sharp as needles. Apparently he took after his sire in that area because coyotes have extremely sharp teeth.

He became a good watchdog, with keen senses and half-breed savagery that won him a healthy respect from all who came in contact with him. But he was gentle with the chickens and other fowls and the small animals on the farm. He was content to lie and sun on the front porch, in collie fashion, and watch the hens and their chicks dusting in the yard. He never killed a chicken or ate an egg, though a coyote would.

If one of the cows or horses was contrary, the dog barked and nipped its heels. And with those sharp teeth, he nearly always drew blood.

Black Pup was a good cattle dog. With patience, we trained him to go to the pasture and bring in the livestock night and morning. Instinctively he followed and herded the animals close to their heels. If one of the cows or horses was contrary, the dog barked and nipped its heels. And with those sharp teeth, he nearly always drew blood. Black Pup learned to avoid the kicking heels by slinking along flat on his belly, quickly nipping and dodging the flailing heels.

When cattle or hogs damaged the fence and strayed where they did not belong, they needed only to hear the yelp of the half-breed and they would scatter back into the pen through the hole in the fence. Black Pup guarded the hole until someone could repair it.

On our farm, chickens wandered about through the pigpens and cow barns, scratching and scavenging for things to eat. Occasionally a brood sow with a vile temper killed a chicken and ate it, and that could become a bad habit. We had such a hog, and we had done everything we could to cure her of the bad habit. We put rings in her snout. Someone said to cut off her tail; and we did that, but nothing stopped her from killing and eating chickens.

Black Pup soon learned that a chicken squawking in the pigpen required investigation. He would yelp and bound for the pen, clear the fence with one leap and tear into the hog with bared teeth. Many times he tore a hunk of hide from the hock of the squealing pig. The hog soon learned that Black Pup was to be feared, and when she heard the yelp, she would release the chicken to avoid those sharp teeth. Eventually she quit eating chickens.

Chickens and eggs were valuable commodities on the farm. The eggs could be sold for cash or traded for staples, and a fat hen always brought cash. Thieves were plentiful. Times where hard, and nomadic humans searching for food or items to turn into ready cash soon learned where the flocks were, and when the farm folks would be gone. One Saturday while we were in town doing our shopping, they came to our place, unmindful of the dog.

He was nearly their match. They only got a few chickens, and only then because they had bruised and hurt Black Pup until he could fight no more. One of his ears was nearly torn off, and although a vet sewed it back on, it didn't stand up like the other after it healed. When we called him and he pricked up his ears, one hung limp in a cocky fashion. But we often wondered how many scars the thieves carried with them.

The dog was a fighter, although he seldom started the argument. He was insanely jealous of any dog that my brother or I petted or showed any affection to. He could lick a dog twice his size. Generally a dog would whimper and limp away with scars for a lifetime from Black Pup.

He was a true hunter. Even though he was short and stocky, he killed at least four coyotes in his 18 years that we knew of. He could catch the gray striped ground squirrel, prairie dogs, tree squirrels and cottontail rabbits. One of his biggest sports was frightening a gray jackrabbit from a brush pile and chasing and playing with it until it was nearly exhausted, like a cat plays with a mouse. Then, just when the poor frightened rabbit was about to give up, Black Pup allowed him to run free and recuperate for another day. Rabbits soon learned to stay away from our farm buildings.

There was a one-dollar bounty on coyotes, and our farm—with its canyons, pastures and hay land— was a perfect place for coyotes. Professional hunters brought their hounds and horses and had a heyday hunting the coyotes on our place. And not only did they get the bounty; coyote hides were worth $5 each, so it was a paying sport. Black Pup loved to go on these hunts and the hunters welcomed him gladly, because he could grab a coyote by the hind legs, roll him over, and the hounds could do the rest.

Eventually his senses dulled and he lost his ability to dodge the flailing hooves of the animals he herded. He received some wicked blows. Several times he lost consciousness, but he never gave up. He finally died at the advanced age of 18 years, succumbing at last to old age and a bad heart.

While dogs and coyotes have been bred and raised for various reasons, I doubt that any could equal our Black Pup. He was a faithful family pet on our Nebraska farm for 18 years while I was growing up. ❖

Leave It to a Mule

By Rex B. Cartwright

ack in northern Wisconsin, where I was born and raised, there was a man who owned a jenny mule. I guess she was as good as any animal. In fact, Jenny had a lot of horse sense to get along with her owner. You might say the same of Tim McShanter; he could get this jenny to do most anything, including work.

Well, Tim owned a stump-pulling rig. I always heard different people say, "This animal is stump broke." I never knew what this meant until Tim told me. "You see, my boy, there ain't every hoss or mule that is stump broke," he said, "which means that it had been trained to work on a stump-pullin' rig like what I got. You come with me tomorrow and I'll show ya."

I was helping old Tim, cultivating his potatoes, when he said this. I was riding Jenny and trying to keep her going straight down the rows. Tim had all he could do to handle the cultivator. In those days, there weren't all of these new-fangled tractor contraptions. I was happy to help Tim cultivate, because I liked to ride Jenny. And then, too, I was earning big wages—10 cents an hour.

Come morning, I was at the McShanter house, bright and early. Even so, Tim was all loaded up and ready to go. Tim had a team of horses to haul his rig around, but he always said that there was no animal that could handle a stump-puller like Jenny. When it came to stump pulling, nobody could beat Jenny and Tim. At least that's what everybody in the community said.

Tim was madder than a wet hen, mostly because he had given away too much of his plug tobacco.

Tim was going to a new farm about four miles away, which we made in nigh onto an hour. Then we started to unload and set up the puller, which to me was a funny contraption. The stump puller worked sort of like the order of our modern winch, only Tim used Jenny for power.

The puller was set on the ground and anchored. Then we put a long pole to the center gear and bolted it in place. On the outer end, we hitched Jenny. Then we ran the cable, wound up on a drum that was on the puller, to one of the stumps to be pulled. Tim fastened the cable to the stump, then going over to where Jenny was, patted her on the neck. All he had to do was say, "Go, Jenny, go!" and she started to make her circle. I held my breath when Jenny came to the cable that ran to the stump, but good old Jenny stepped over it just as spry as a kitten. Yes, sir, I reckon that's what you call stump broke.

Every round the cable eased the stump out just a little; every few rounds, Jenny would stop. I never did rightly know if she wanted a rest or she just wanted that little hunk of brown mule chewing tobacco that Tim gave her. I heard somebody tried to give her some horseshoe plug tobacco and she turned it down.

The day wore on and so did Tim's plug of brown mule tobacco. Every time Tim went stump pulling, there always came a crowd of spectators, and when he took out his chewing tobacco, they would all mooch a hunk of it. By mid-afternoon, Tim ran out of plug and good old Jenny stopped with just two stumps to go.

Tim went over to Jenny and patted her on the neck, which did no good. Then he grabbed the bridle and tried to lead that mule. That just made Jenny mad. She sat down, threw her head back and let out a big "Hee-haw!" Right then, Tim got an idea and spat out the chaw in his mouth. He gave it to Jenny. She seemed satisfied, because she got up and started her merry-go-round again. By collecting chews from the spectators, we got the stump pulled. We were going strong on the last stump when all of the "secondhand" tobacco gave out.

Tim was madder than a wet hen, mostly because he had given away too much of his plug tobacco. Then someone hauled out a can of Copenhagen snuff, with the suggestion that he try to get Jenny going with it. Tim took a little in his hand and held it out to Jenny who sniffed and snorted; then she took it and started on her way.

Did you ever take a chew of snuff? It sure has what you call "it." Jenny threw her head up and every round she went a little faster. Tim began to yell "Whoa!" but it did him no good. Finally, coming to the cable, instead of stepping over it, she jumped over it.

By now, Tim was running in toward Jenny and yelling like a wild man. And the stump—it was coming out fast with only one big root holding. Tim made a headlong dive at Jenny, and she must have tried to get away by giving a big jump. Right then that root gave way. The stump flew through the air, carrying a couple of hundred pounds of dirt with it. The stump went smack-dab into the puller, knocking it loose from its anchor. Dirt flew through the air, hitting Tim amidship, knocking him flat. Jenny made one desperate lunge for freedom and made it. She took off through the brush, braying at the top of her voice, heading straight for home.

We had a lot of help, which was mostly advice, but by sundown we had the cable back on the drum, the puller loaded up on the wagon, and we were headed for home.

Perhaps it was the rum that had been added to the Copenhagen, or perhaps it was only its natural ingredients. At any rate, Tim was going to kill that Jenny when he got home. But he didn't. Another thing he never did—he never gave Jenny any more Copenhagen snuff, and as far as I know, that stump-broke mule never had another runaway. ❖

The Man Behind the Plow

Author Unknown

I'm not so much at singing as you high falutin' chaps,
My voice is kind of husky and a little loud perhaps
For I have been a-plowin' with a lazy team, you see,
They keep me rather busy, with my "gid-dap, whoa, haw, gee,"
But if you'll pay attention I have just a word to say,
About a great mistake they make and do it every day,
In dealing out your praise, and if this you will allow,
Too often do you slight the man, who walks behind the plow.

Chorus:
You talk about your learned men, their wit and wisdom rare,
Your poets, and your painters, they get praises everywhere
They are well enough to make a show, but can you tell me how
This world would ever do without the "man behind the plow?"

It's well enough to go to school and learn to read and write,
It's nicer still to dress up fine and sport around at night.
Your music, painting, poetry are very hard to beat,
But tell me what you're gonna do for something good to eat?
You say my boots are muddy and my clothing rather coarse,
I make a good companion for the oxen and the horse
My face is red, my hands are hard; 'tis true, I will allow,
But don't you be too quick to spurn the man behind the plow.

Your buyers, clerks and businessmen with fingers white and small
And men of each profession, but the farmer feeds them all,
If he should quit his business, there would be an awful row
The world could not exist without the man behind the plow.
There is the city dude you know a-trippin' with his cane,
His hands are soft and white as snow but then, Ah! what of him,
He is nothing but a parasite and this you will allow,
He couldn't hold a candle to the boy behind the plow.

I like your great inventions and I'm glad you're gettin' smart.
I like to hear your music for it kinda cheers my heart,
But it can not fill the stomach of a real hungry man,
But I've called your attention to the kind of thing that can,
Now boys don't be too eager for to quit the good old farm,
Your father's strength is failing, soon he'll need your faithful arm,
If you're honest in your purpose, at your feet the world will bow,
For the Greatest of all Great Men is the Man Behind the Plow.